I have tried to uphold the values that America has always stood for—that every individual has worth and is entitled to respect and justice and fundamental freedoms, and to seek to fulfill their potential.

SENATOR SAM NUNN
Georgia

All values are important, everyone who has ever touched my life in some way was a mentor for good or bad.

GENERAL COLIN POWELL
Former Chairman, Joint Chiefs of Staff

I would want to be remembered first for being a good family man and for raising five children in an environment that emphasized family values.

DON SHULA
The Miami Dolphins

I have underlying respect for the broad-shouldered family man and woman who care more about their kids than themselves, and they are willing to make sacrifices so that their children can succeed.

FRANK BORMAN
Former Astronaut

The good that you do will come back to you and it really doesn't cost very much.

DAVID PACKARD
Founder, Hewlett-Packard

Without values, nations, societies and individuals can pitch straight to hell.

JAMES MICHENER
Author

My father taught me to be results-oriented and never to give up. My mother taught me compassion, love and patience.

J. W. MARRIOTT, JR.
Marriott Corporation

I'd like to be remembered for my integrity, generosity, and for courage in the face of adversity.

ANN LANDERS
Syndicated Columnist

Ambassador Capen was especially prepared to be a great envoy because he has a thoroughgoing knowledge of Hispanic roots of the great American nation.

MANUEL FRAGA IRIBARNE
President of Galicia
"Father" of Modern Spain

I strive for uncommon excellence in all that I do, although it remains a distant goal.

TOM JOHNSON
President, CNN

In Richard Capen are combined with magnificent results, the facets of diplomacy and journalism which he has brilliantly exercised throughout his life. He continued being a consummate connoisseur of Spanish reality.

LIEUTENANT GENERAL SABINO FERNANDEZ CAMPO
Former Chief of Staff
His Majesty the King of Spain

I learned from my father the value of absolute integrity and the steady insistence on racial tolerance decades before this was an acceptable attitude in a small southern community.

TERRY SANFORD
Former Governor of North Carolina

My personal philosophy is quite simple. I am responsible for me and must oversee with great sensitivity the impact of what I say and/or do on others.

BARBARA JORDAN
Former Congresswoman

Some men and women make the world better just by being the kind of people they are.

JOHN GARDNER
Founder of Common Cause

I want to be remembered for providing a sense of perspective—an awareness that many of the things that society tends to get wrought up about are in fact trivial or silly.

DAVE BARRY
Newspaper Columnist

One of my most important accomplishments, one I am still working on, is to be a huge success in the grandfather business.

FORMER PRESIDENT GEORGE BUSH

I would like to be remembered for being an honest person who tried to do his best and enjoyed life to the fullest.

SENATOR BARRY GOLDWATER
Arizona

Nothing in life prepares you for the challenge or the reward of raising two fine children in a difficult world. Compared to them Regis is a cinch.

KATHIE LEE GIFFORD
Live—Regis & Kathie Lee

George Bush taught me that if you try your hardest, are decent and honest, you can do anything you want.

BARBARA BUSH

We must honor and preserve the most important institution in America—the very foundation of our society—the family.

GOVERNOR PETE WILSON
California

Freedom is a process in which we are all involved—nonstop.

MARVIN KALB
Harvard Professor and Former Newscaster

Finish Strong

Living Your Faith in the Secular World
& Inspiring Others in the Process

Finish Strong

Revised and Expanded Edition

Richard G. Capen, Jr.

This Billy Graham Evangelistic Association
special edition is published with permission
from ZondervanPublishingHouse.

HarperSanFrancisco/Zondervan
An Imprint of HarperCollins*Publishers*

Grateful acknowledgment is made to the following for permission to reprint copy-righted material: From *Selected Poems* published by Bloodaxe Books Ltd., Newcastle-upon-Tyne. Copyright © Jenny Joseph 1992. (U.S. distributors: Oufours Press.)

HarperCollins Web Site: http://www.harpercollins.com
HarperCollins®, 📖®, and HarperSanFrancisco™
are trademarks of HarperCollins Publishers Inc.
Zondervan Publishers Web Site: http://www.zondervan.com

ISBN 0-913367-91-5

With Gratitude

To Joan, who has filled my life with unconditional love, a strong Christian faith, and untiring compassion for family and friends. For thirty-seven years she has been my caring partner and wise counselor, especially during those times when I have needed encouragement or strong doses of humility.

In dedicating this book to her, I include our children, who, after years of learning from us, have become our role models and best friends. We love them for all that they have done to enrich everything important in our lives:

To Chris, our book-publishing son, who has exemplified the virtues of hard work and persistence in pursuing with enthusiasm the creation of his own business.

To Kelly, our attorney-daughter, who throughout her life has shown determination and commitment, and exceptionally good judgment in marrying J. D. Douglas, a wonderful addition to our family. Much to our great joy, they have presented us with our first grandchild, a daughter, Courtney Capen Douglas.

To Carrie, the talented and creative genius of our clan, who has reminded us to appreciate our many blessings and to know that the most important things in life are not found on the bottom line but in the love we share. We are grateful to her for bringing into our family her husband, James Hasler, a bright young electrical engineer.

A Note to Readers

The author welcomes comments and questions from readers of *Finish Strong*. He may be reached as follows:

Dick Capen
Box 2494
Rancho Santa Fe, California 92067

Fax: (619) 756-1857
E-mail: rgcapen@aol.com

With Admiration

*I cannot take credit for whatever God has
chosen to accomplish through us and our
ministry; only God deserves the glory, and
we can never thank Him enough for the
great things He has done.*

BILLY GRAHAM *(Just As I Am)*

*Whatever else, Lord, you're about,
You have not finished with us
—yet.*

RUTH GRAHAM *(By My Laughing Fire)*

My personal friendship with Ruth and Billy Graham goes back to
1969 when they came to the Pentagon to help us dedicate a newly constructed meditation room created by secretary of defense Mel Laird for
use by the some 25,000 employees who worked there. We had just
inherited a terribly divisive war in Vietnam, and the power of prayer
was essential to us all.

Subsequently, Billy helped us bring hope to the families of prisoners
of war and missing in action during my own service in the Defense
Department. Years later, after my 1992 Senate confirmation as U.S.
ambassador to Spain, he officiated at my swearing in ceremony at the
State Department in Washington.

One never forgets any meeting with this gentle man of God. The
inspiring power of his ministry, mixed with an impeccable reputation
as the world's most respected human being, engulf the room. To accept

him *"Just As I Am"* (the title of his recently released autobiography) is impossible. Save that for the One who has blessed us with his ministry for over a half-century.

Ruth and Billy have been in our home. They have spoken to my colleagues in the newspaper publishing business. I have prayed with them on dozens of occasions, including the National Prayer Breakfast which Billy started with President Dwight Eisenhower in 1953.

In 1976 Billy allowed me the privilege of serving as co-chairman for a Billy Graham Bicentennial Crusade held that year in San Diego, and I have served on the Billy Graham Evangelistic Association Board of Directors since 1990.

As a director of the Billy Graham Evangelistic Association (BGEA), I have seen firsthand the incredible force of his ministry, in which he has preached to over 100 million people in person and 2 billion worldwide via radio, television, satellites circling the globe and other media.

Since the start of his ministry in 1945, his faithfulness to the Gospel message has remained absolutely constant. And, alongside, is Ruth, an articulate and committed missionary in her own right. This loving wife and caring mother has led her own unsung ministry with good humor, great insight and uncommon courage.

I am honored that the Grahams' colleagues at the BGEA have selected *Finish Strong* for this special edition. To God goes all the glory.

With great humility and appreciation, I dedicate this edition to Ruth and Billy Graham, who have inspired in my family an eternal love of God in Jesus Christ.

With the blessing of our Lord, they have shown us all how to finish strong every day.

Contents

Foreword

When I worked in Florida I met a true-life American hero. Richard Capen was publisher of the Pulitzer Prize–winning *Miami Herald*. As such he found himself forced to serve as referee between warring factions of that city. The immigrant Cuban population declared a special war against Capen and his paper, and talk radio incited the Hispanics even further. On two occasions mobs marched on the newspaper headquarters to burn it down. On two other occasions African Americans were inflamed against Cubans, and citywide riots ensued.

Capen stood his ground. He took private lessons to learn Spanish and became a champion of Cuban interests. He performed wonders in alleviating African American animosities. And he maintained the integrity and profitability of his newspaper. This man fought the battles without losing his temper or taking prejudiced sides, displaying responsible citizenship at a noble level.

I was delighted when President Bush appointed him ambassador to Spain, where he covered himself with glory and the dust of sixty-five different Spanish cities that he visited to show the American flag and his deep interest in things Spanish.

This book ably summarizes his attitudes and beliefs. It will prove a good read.

James A. Michener
Austin, Texas

Ruth and I will never forget the first time we met Dick Capen. At the time he was deputy assistant secretary of defense, and he invited us to meet with the American prisoners of war returning from Vietnam. It was a deeply moving experience to talk with these courageous men, many of whom told us how their faith in God had sustained them during their darkest days.

As I watched Dick warmly welcome them back to America, I began to realize that he was one of the most gifted and yet compassionate men I had ever met. Since that time I have watched him become one of America's most distinguished newspaper publishers and public servants. More than that, I have come to esteem him as a valued personal friend and adviser.

This book summarizes the principles that have guided Dick's life. As he rightly stresses, inner character must always be the wellspring and foundation for our outward actions. Without that commitment to a strong inner character, our lives will inevitably fall short. No one can help but profit from Dick Capen's insights.

Dr. Billy Graham
Montreat, North Carolina

Dick Capen served his country well. First, he exemplified the very highest standards in his profession of journalism. Then, he served with distinction as ambassador to Spain. Now, through this book, he possibly has accomplished his most important work: an honest discussion of the importance of character and morality and what it means to the future of America. We salute Dick for having the courage to undertake this project, and we are very proud to call him our friend.

George and Barbara Bush
Houston, Texas

On the Record

My years as publisher of *The Miami Herald* and as a public servant provided unusual access to special people from all walks of life. Some ran grocery stores, others ran the country. Some had enormous energy, others were crippled and bedridden. All have accomplished exceptional things in their lives.

As I gathered material for this book, I decided to conduct a survey of these wonderful friends and acquaintances. My survey consisted of four questions:

- What three accomplishments do you consider to be the most important in your life?
- If you knew you were going to die tomorrow, what two or three values would you want to be remembered for?
- Who have been your mentors, and what did they teach you?
- Name an unsung hero whose values you admire.

When more than 80 percent responded, I knew I was onto something special. For one thing, I had touched some sensitive nerves. Some called and asked for more time. A few said the survey was so personal they could not deal with it. Others said the questions had stimulated family debate and some very painful reflection. More than a few said the exercise had caused them to set new priorities.

Sadly, eight leaders died before they could read their responses in this book. One had put together his barely legible answers just weeks before he died. Another, former chief justice Warren Burger, had set his survey aside hoping to respond when he recovered from a serious bout of pneumonia, but he never did.

Two had been important to my career: Dave Packard, who was Mel

Laird's key deputy in the Pentagon and one of the most modest people I have ever met; and Jim Batten, the much-respected chief executive and my close friend at Knight Ridder. Then there was Dewey Knight, the highest ranking black official in Miami and the person who introduced me to the soul of the inner city. The worst blow of all came with Harry Jenkins's accidental death (see chapter 10).

These good people remind us that it is never too soon to set the key priorities in our lives because tomorrow may be too late.

Some of the surveys were answered in the midst of defining moments: General Colin Powell as he and his family anguished over whether he should run for president; Senator Sam Nunn as he was wrapping up his decision to retire from the United States Senate.

I knew that something very special would come from people like Marine Corps General Jim Lawrence, whose wise counsel as my deputy in the Pentagon kept me out of trouble, and *The Miami Herald's* Dave Barry, whose counsel was outrageous. Then there was Alvah Chapman, who recruited me for Knight Ridder and kept me challenged for thirteen years. The thoughtful responses from Bill Marriott and Tom Phillips (former CEO at Raytheon) were what you'd expect from two of the most honorable business leaders I have ever met. Rabbi Lehrman introduced me to the concept of ethical wills (see chapter 4). Not many Christian publishers have their own rabbi and so I was especially proud to call him mine.

It came as no surprise that many of the most respected leaders in the survey were the most humble in describing their accomplishments. Stripped away from their comments were superficial public images and any transitory trappings of office. They spoke through the heart, not through some sterile press release.

A few prove the adage that you are never too old to take on new adventures: Barry Goldwater, who finally saw the pursuit of virtue a reality; John Gardner, who's out there leading a crusade to renew our communities; Billy Graham, who is preaching to millions via satellite; and Jim Michener, who at age eighty-nine was working on a book about values.

In all the survey replies, a common thread occurred: the influence of dedicated parents and family, faith in God, and hard work. Nearly all referred in one way or another to the American Dream and how it had helped them: modest roots, the freedom to succeed if they worked hard, the joy of achievement, the humility of failure, and the determination to end up on top. Though many could rest on their laurels, few were; they had a compulsion to share with others and to make the world a better place.

You will find the results of this survey throughout the pages of this book. Most are identified as "On the Record" sidebars. Others may be found in the text itself. I hope you find them as inspiring as I did. And I hope they might prompt you to consider your own answers.

It could be your next step in your continuing effort to finish strong.

Introduction

Dick, above all, finish strong.
GEORGE BUSH
The White House
January 5, 1993

It was a cold January morning four thousand miles from the White House when the president's letter arrived at my embassy office in Madrid. In a few days George Bush would be turning over his responsibilities and, shortly thereafter, I would be leaving my job as ambassador. He knew it would be tempting for his ambassadors around the world just to coast until he left office. Coasting was unacceptable to President Bush.

My wife, Joan, and I had first met Barbara and George Bush in the late 1960s when he was a freshman congressman and I was in the Pentagon as special assistant to the secretary of defense, Mel Laird. That experience proved invaluable years later after President Bush sent my name to the Congress for Senate confirmation as an ambassador for my country. It was important to achieve bipartisan support in the U.S. Senate for my nomination. And with the help of friends on both sides of the aisle, the Senate vote was unanimous, both within the Foreign Relations Committee and from the full Senate. My predecessor had narrowly won the committee vote by a margin of ten to nine, and I was grateful that I could begin my career as ambassador free of such disputes.

Serving as an American ambassador seemed a wonderful way to top off a thirty-year career in the newspaper business. The job was a perfect fit because so many of my experiences in government and newspapers could be useful as a diplomat. I had lived most of my life in two regions steeped with Spanish culture—Southern California and Miami. I had deep admiration for George and Barbara Bush and for the personal values they reflected. I also had strongly supported the president's foreign policy and shared his commitment to use key embassies to promote economic opportunities for the United States.

My personal ties to Spain were important too. After thirteen years in Miami, we were reasonably conversant in Spanish. Joan had studied in Barcelona in the late 1950s as a college student, and our older daughter, Kelly, had lived there twice—once as a high-school summer student residing with a wonderful family in a small coastal community in northern Spain and later as a college student for a semester abroad at the University of Madrid.

In 1992 our son, Chris, published a book on the America's Cup competition, and one of the six foreign-language editions was distributed in Spanish in honor of Spain's entry in the yachting competition. Our younger daughter, Carrie, was then in college majoring in art history. Before we left, she became our personal tutor on Spain's priceless collection of art.

The timing of my appointment was ideal. Nineteen ninety-two was the Year of Spain; packed into one year were the Barcelona Summer Olympic Games, the world's fair (Expo) in Sevilla, and the designation of Madrid as that year's cultural capital of Europe. When I arrived in Madrid, U.S. relations with Spain were at an all-time high. After Iraq's invasion of Kuwait, Spain had volunteered its bases in the Allied cause. This was in marked contrast to years of bitter negotiations with antimilitary elements in the Socialist government over the presence of U.S. forces in Spain. As it turned out, Operation Desert Storm was actually launched in Spain with the American B-52s flying from the Torrejón air base outside Madrid.

It Was God's Will

As Joan and I thought about this important career move, we prayed for guidance. As exciting the task, it was going to be difficult to leave behind our family and to realize that the demands of the ambassadorship would likely be overwhelming at times.

We thanked God for this unique privilege to serve, and we knew it was His will that so many of our interests and experiences had converged in such a powerful way.

John 3:27 came to mind: "God in heaven appoints each [person's] work" (TLB).

The opportunity to make a genuine contribution on behalf of my country and my personal ties with Spain were very much on my mind as I rode down the streets of Old Madrid in an eighteenth-century horse-drawn carriage sent by the king. Dressed in a traditional diplomat's morning jacket and white tie, I was on my way to present my credentials at the Royal Palace, just as our first ambassador to Spain, Ben Franklin, had done two hundred years earlier. Preceding me en route were more than one hundred Spanish soldiers colorfully dressed in eighteenth-century uniforms; they were on horseback and accompanied by a military band.

At the precise moment the gold-trimmed chariot turned into the huge, marble-paved courtyard of the king's official headquarters, Palacio Real, a fifty-member royal band, standing at attention near the palace entrance, saluted my arrival with the playing of our country's national anthem. It was a very dramatic moment for a kid from Queens, New York.

The king's protocol officer, who met the carriage at the entrance, escorted me up two expansive flights of marble stairs lined with colorfully dressed *alabarderos,* the palace royal guards who were holding ceremonial swords. After passing through a half-dozen huge palace rooms decorated with gold-gilded ceilings and deep-purple velvet walls, I entered the official reception hall where ambassadors are presented to His Majesty. I stopped a few feet in front of King Juan Carlos. Off to my right were three senior embassy officers, including my deputy chief of mission. In my left hand was a handwritten note from President Bush and the family Bible used when I had taken my oath of office in Washington a few days earlier. Joan stood in the anteroom nearby with Flora Rosal Bertrand, an eighty-year-old Spanish *viuda* (widow) from Barcelona who thirty-eight years earlier had cared for my wife, then a young teenage exchange student in Spain.

Spain is one of the few countries in the world to maintain this spectacular royal tradition for welcoming new ambassadors. First came a few formal words of greeting: the king spoke in perfect English while I offered some well-rehearsed words in Spanish. We then adjourned to a small office where we exchanged personal greetings and discussed our mutual respect for George and Barbara Bush. I asked King Juan Carlos if he would sign my family Bible in honor of the occasion. This was a very special, leather-bound edition presented to me by Billy Graham in 1976 when I served as chairman of his Bicentennial Crusade in San Diego.

Sharing My Family Bible

I pointed to the page where President Bush and others had signed earlier and passed His Majesty the pen I had borrowed from my defense attaché. In horror, I watched the king struggle in vain to sign the book. The colonel's pen was out of ink. Somewhat panicked, I blurted out the observation that if this had been a treaty-signing ceremony, I would have flunked the course. Juan Carlos was a gracious host with a good sense of humor. As His Majesty left the room to find his own pen, I thought how much that Air Force colonel who had provided me his was going to enjoy the next tour . . . in Siberia. My Bible still shows deep indentations where King Juan Carlos tried repeatedly to make that cheap U.S. government–issue pen work. After fifteen minutes, the ceremony ended and my diplomatic career had been launched. Short of a coronation, I had become an ambassador about as dramatically as any government career could ever begin.

As this incredible ceremony came to a close, I couldn't help reflecting back on my modest roots, growing up in New York City. With no money for college, I had won a scholarship to study at Columbia University, served in the Navy, and almost by sheer luck landed in the newspaper business. The American Dream had been very good to me and I was eager to serve my country once again, this time in Spain.

We packed a lot into our brief term of service. In less than a year, we had shown the flag in sixty-seven cities in all seventeen autonomous regions of Spain and entertained more than seven thousand guests at our embassy residence. Too soon, however, it was time to return to the States, so we packed our bags and returned not to Miami but to Southern California. We decided before going to Spain that it was time to go "home" — back to the state where Joan and I had met and married and where all three of our children were born.

Putting Our Trust in Him

The Lord had blessed us in so many ways and we wanted to be reunited with our family and devote more time to serving others. We trusted in God, prayed daily for guidance and found comfort in His way.

Joan was anxious to resume her graduate studies in theology and our move to Southern California, where Westminster Presbyterian Seminary is located, would make that possible.

After thirty years in the newspaper business and government service, I wanted to finish strong and devote my time to reflection and writing about troubling trends I began to see developing during my years with *The Miami Herald* and in public service. What concerned me was that things just aren't right in our country.

While there is so much good to celebrate, there also are too many disturbing trends to worry us. You know the list: crime, breakdown of the family, leaders we can't trust, a general loss of faith in "the system," poverty, racism, drugs, and the like. As a community we seem to have lost our way. People are confused, and very frustrated.

Actually, these trends are just symptoms. The real problem lies deep within each of us. It is the cumulative effect of the gradual erosion of values that has left us as a nation without a moral rudder. Our country has been losing its moral and spiritual roots for some time, and the result is that our souls are in pain.

As I began putting my concerns on paper, I recalled George Bush's final words of advice to me. While he was referring specifically to the way I should conclude my term as ambassador, it seemed like pretty good advice for all of us. Think of the many times you have had a good idea, a noble intention, a New Year's resolution, a plan of action—but somehow it never amounted to anything. In a way, that's where I think we are in terms of our personal values. We have good intentions but let them slip. We know what's right, but we do not follow through. We know the words, but not the deeds. We do not set a steady course. We start off with good intentions, but we too often get sidetracked.

It's time not only to take stock, but to recommit ourselves to what is good and helpful, and then finish strong.

It is not for me to prescribe a list of values that, if embraced by everyone, will put this nation back on course. But I do hope to make you think about what really matters most to you—those beliefs and values that you know are right—and encourage you to stay true to them and then act upon them. Together, we must not fail in this task if we are to survive as a nation.

I am an optimist, and always have been. The majority of Americans are good people who desire to make the world a better place. We have not given up. Rather, we have hope, compassion, and confidence that we can restore balance in life. We know what's right, and we are amazingly resilient. I know because, as the publisher of a metropolitan newspaper and, on two occasions, as a public servant, I've had the privilege to view a broad spectrum of good people. I will tell their stories and I will share some of my own to help you see what it takes to finish strong in everything you do.

I also will share the fascinating results of a personal survey I conducted with some well-known leaders that I respect. What they have to say is included in each chapter in an "On the Record" feature. You will recognize many names and you will see, over and over again, that values matter in real life.

Most of all, you will be reminded throughout this book that you are not alone. There are millions out there just like you. People who want strong families, safe neighborhoods, and a decent world in which our children can prosper. We are tired of quick fixes that don't work, of broken promises made by inept politicians. We want solid change for the long haul, not phony pledges that will fade after the election. The truth is: real change is up to us.

Several years ago, a visitor to Mother Teresa's Calcutta mission was nearly overcome by the task she faced and asked her, "How do you possibly hope to feed all the hungry people who come to your mission?" Her response is a reminder of the power each of us has: "One mouth at a time." That's how we will improve our country too—one person, one couple, one family, one community at a time.

And it will start with you.

Finish Strong

Chapter 1

Faith

From Your Beliefs Come Values

Having a position of power does not bring inner security and fulfillment. That comes only by developing a personal relationship with God, which for me is personified by Jesus Christ. Inner security and fulfillment comes by faith—not by wielding power in the town where power is king.

When I look back on my own journey of faith I can see that real growth began when I started reading God's Word as a young man. I really do believe that those of us who are put in positions of public trust really shouldn't be hesitant to speak about spiritual values.

SECRETARY OF STATE JAMES BAKER
1990 National Prayer Breakfast

Faith Keeper

Life is not just a few years to spend on self-indulgence and career advancement. It's a privilege, a responsibility, a stewardship to be lived according to a much higher calling—God's calling. This alone gives true meaning to life.

ELIZABETH DOLE
President, The American Red Cross

As I reflect on the various chapters of my life and career, I am overwhelmed by a gracious God who has blessed and guided me every step of the way.

My Christian faith defines who I am, and it is the foundation of my marriage and family. Faith has been essential to my careers in public service and newspaper publishing. My beliefs provide the underpinning for every important personal value. For me, that dependence upon God as the compass of my life is personified through His Son, Jesus Christ, who trusted in the will of His Father.

In all candor, I cannot cite a specific moment when I accepted the Lord as my Savior, but I do know that my faith in Him has grown stronger every year. God has had a plan for me even when I did not always acknowledge His presence. He has been at my side even when I didn't hold Him first among my own selfish priorities.

I have been blessed in so many ways: challenging and exciting careers in government and the media, a loving family, a solid education, good health, and unique opportunities to uplift key values essential in life.

Each move in my career seemed to be a magical combination of all that I had learned to date, merged together for greater good. With gratitude, I acknowledge those circumstances as God's will for me.

Over the years, I have been deeply influenced by some wonderful faith mentors, starting with my wife, Joan, who has been at my side for over thirty-seven years. Together we have been blessed with three wonderful children, now supplemented by two terrific sons-in-law and our first grandchild.

Another mentor in molding my faith has been Dan Yeary during the years when he was senior pastor at University Baptist Church in Miami. Dan, who now heads a huge church in North Phoenix, inspired our entire family with his strong ministry uniquely tailored to South Florida's vast diversity. His sermons, offered simultaneously in two languages, were convincing and uplifting. The Capen family is extremely grateful for the many ways this gentle man of God has enriched our Christian journey.

Other key mentors for our faith are celebrated throughout this book. Many talk openly about how their faith has been central to every good thing they have done.

Most of us survive today in a secular world where we are surrounded by the unchurched and disbelievers. It can be a very tough and frustrating dilemma. Yet, separating our faith from the rest of life is not an option.

Some of the best opportunities we have to help others understand the promise of God come in completely secular settings. I am convinced that this has been one of the most important of the Lord's missions for me.

So many around have an urgent need to hear the Word but never go to church. They seldom experience the power of prayer and they know little about the joy that comes simply by accepting the presence of God.

Sharing our faith outside the comfort of Sunday service is key, according to Bill Armstrong, former United States senator from Colorado. He puts the challenge in this way:

Faith Keeper

Jesus lived among everyday people, just as we do. He spoke to them of life and death issues in mundane settings. And, He did not wait for people to come to Him. He went to them.

No matter what the environment, we are provided some very important opportunities to reflect the faith of God in all that we do. Many times, we are the only "bible" some people will ever experience so our personal example is a very important testimony of Christian love.

We may not be able to change the corrupt character of others but we can live our own lives in ways that give honor to His name.

Above all, we simply cannot live by one set of Personal Values in the office, and then shift to other standards on Sunday. Consistent Christian commitment is absolutely key. So, what can you do? Well, here are a few headlines:

Make prayer a key part of your life.

In times of crisis, I always turn to God in prayer asking for strength to deal with issues that need resolving. Whenever I faced a career move, my wife and I turned to Him in prayer.

Our friends and family should be encouraged to pray too. And read the Bible. In both San Diego and Miami, I helped start men's Bible study groups. Each created wonderful, lifelong friendships among the leaders involved. One group has been meeting every other Friday for more than 25 years.

Thousands of Bible study groups exist in the country, including your community; they represent a powerful force in America today.

From the moment I entered high school, I asked for the Lord's help in finding a way to pay for college. On the way to church for my own wedding, I stopped before a huge cross mounted atop the highest point in San Diego to pray for His blessings on my marriage.

When the newly appointed secretary of defense, Mel Laird, called to ask if I would join his team at the Pentagon, we prayed for guidance in our decision. Before we accepted an important career move to South Florida, we met with two of our children in the privacy of our hotel room in Miami so that we could ask Him to bless our adventure, and He did.

Often, the demands of my job as publisher of *The Miami Herald* forced me into the office at 5 or 6 A.M. on Friday so that I could complete my Sunday column before the crisis of the day erupted. As the sun would rise, I would pray for guidance and vision so that I could give hope to the readers of our newspaper. Sometimes, I was as discouraged as those I was needing to uplift and, in those troubling circumstances, it took His help to get there. Proverbs 3:5–6 often gave me the lift I needed:

> *Trust the Lord completely; don't ever trust yourself. In everything you do, put God first, and he will direct you and crown your efforts with success* (TLB).

Witness to His Word

For almost forty years, I have been involved in career assignments that required my very best, ethical leadership. Above all, such responsibilities demanded that I live out my Christian faith through personal example.

This doesn't mean I have carried religion on my sleeve. Quite to the contrary. I have found many opportunities—almost every day—to reflect my values and faith without turning off those who may differ from me.

If they really thought about it, the people who worked with or for me over the years would know full well where I was coming from as I dealt with business and public policy issues.

When I was sworn in as my country's ambassador to Spain, my wife and I asked Billy Graham and U.S. Senate Chaplain Dick Halverson to participate in the ceremony at the State Department. We wanted to start our duties with prayer. It was an important statement of our faith, and of our gratitude for the privilege God had given us.

We chose that day a special New Testament reading that we felt captured the sense of our new career as diplomats:

> We are Christ's ambassadors. God is using us to speak to you (2 Corinthians 5:20, TLB).

Just remember. Someone out there is watching your every move. Your personal example may be the only witness to the Lord that person ever experiences.

Be an Encourager

Little in life is possible without the uplifting power of encouragement, even when there is little reason to be encouraged.

We are blessed with ways to give hope to others every day. A pat on the back. A simple hello. A quiet expression of concern. To be an encourager is one of the most powerful New Testament messages. Here's what Paul has to say:

> Are your hearts tender and sympathetic at all? Then make me truly happy by loving each other and agreeing whole-

*heartedly with each other, working together with one heart
and mind and purpose.... Be humble, thinking of others as
better than yourself. Don't just think about your own
affairs, but be interested in others, too, and in what they are
doing. (Philippians 2:1–4, TLB).*

Theologist William Barclay put this important message this way:

*One of the highest of human duties is the duty of encourage-
ment... It is easy to laugh at men's ideals; it is easy to pour
cold water on their enthusiasm; it is easy to discourage others.
The world is full of discouragers. Many a time a word of
praise or thanks or appreciation or cheer has kept a man on
his feet. Blessed is the man who speaks such a word.*

Be True to Your Beliefs

In the end, there is no way we can be all things to all people. So, the
answer is profoundly simple: Be clear in who you are and set your life
to follow a moral compass that never waivers.

If you are to reflect God's will, it's important to have it in focus—all
the time. Then, you can inspire others without turning them off while
they search for answers to life's meaning.

Living in a painfully divided city, there was absolutely no way I could
satisfy everyone all the time. I couldn't even reach that goal within my
own family! I learned early on that any belief worth having in life is likely to be controversial, and so be it. Just remember one thing: You have
the right to hold your beliefs and to be respected for doing so.

The key here is to *live* the walk, not just talk about it.

Be a Missionary in Your Own Town

Management consultant Ken Blanchard puts it this way:

Faith Keeper

The Bible tells us that everyone in the family of God is a minister—we just do not necessarily have to run a church or move to another country.

Each day we are given dozens of opportunities to reflect our faith by showing the gentleness that Jesus has taught us. It may be nothing more than our quiet demeanor with a perfect stranger, someone who is desperately looking for hope or encouragement, and we don't even know it.

As we uplift the good examples of others, we hold up their good values for the rest of the world to admire. Through that process, we teach the world what is needed to bring about a caring society built on mutual respect.

For every disbeliever in life, there are dozens who are looking for answers. Such people are more than willing to at least consider the powerful message of God, and that is where you come in.

As Christians, we have an obligation to be missionaries in all that we do. How can others know the Word through you if they never hear it from you?

Adjust Your Priorities to God's Priorities

Sorting through key decisions in life can be a painful experience: where to go to college, which job to take, who to marry, where to live, how to raise your kids. Many choices involve trade-offs. Sometimes we must move away from our comfort zone, giving up good friends and past successes. And, woven through it all, are tests of our own integrity and what we believe is ultimately important in our lives.

How essential are the trappings of your life? Are there new mountains to climb? Are you stretching yourself, using your God-given energies and talents to the fullest?

Does the Lord really want you to coast, to rest on your laurels, to live the good life at the expense of serving others? Just remember that He expects us to use our talents wisely, no matter how young, no matter how old, and He demands the utmost of our effort and integrity.

I was present at the 1990 National Prayer Breakfast in Washington when former secretary of state Jim Baker spoke about his faith and dependency on God (see his quote at the beginning of this chapter). He later told me that this talk generated more comments than any other talk he had ever delivered.

His was an important testimony, even as he dealt with his own frail-ties. "I am just one person genuinely struggling to put faith into practice in my life," he said. Isn't that true for all of us?

Putting our faith into practice is not just the Lord's gift to us. It's our responsi-bility to Him. It's His priority for us.

On the surface many Americans may appear to be disinterested in the scandals swirling around these days, but no one should underestimate their commitment to the fundamental values of life.

The importance of integrity and faith remain strong everywhere I go. And that, in my opinion, remains a powerful story waiting to be told.

Under my watch at *The Miami Herald*, we asked one of our most respected staff writers, John Dorschner, to spend the bet-ter part of a year visiting churches, cathe-drals, and synagogues in South Florida.

> ## On the Record
>
> *My parents were my most impor-tant mentors. They always tithed, always went to church, and always took responsibility for doing their part in whatever needed to be done in the church and the community.*
>
> SENATOR SAM NUNN
> Democrat, Georgia
>
> *Would we behave as we behave in word, thought and deed if we unconditionally believed that we are God's stewards performing His work?*
>
> BARBARA JORDAN
> Former congresswoman
> and college professor

Our reporter was shocked at what he found: a huge world of unreport-ed news and feature stories involving thousands of dedicated people of all faiths who were doing important and interesting things.

"People have a hunger for religion news and there's plenty out there that's not being reported," Dorschner said in a critique I asked him to prepare. Because he was addressing his newsroom colleagues, the writer was understandably low-key, but no one could have missed the point. I wouldn't have been so tactful. Most newspapers do a lousy job with their religion beat.

There are dozens of stories out there that matter deeply in the lives of readers, and our dailies are missing far too many of them. Dorschner complained that untrained young reporters were assigned religion news but that most knew little about the subject and disliked having to write about it. In some newspapers, religion news is relegated to the Friday section "ghetto," as Dorschner described it. In others, the news runs on Saturdays back with the classified ads, too late to be of any help for those who try to plan ahead for their weekend activities.

While the media coverage has stepped up some in the past year or two, it's spotty at best and often written by those unqualified to cover the story. And I don't mean to limit criticism to newspapers; television and weekly magazines do even less.

Pick up your Sunday or Monday morning newspaper and you will find it's loaded with page after page of sports stories covering every last detail of the games played. But I defy you to find anything more than a column or two about the thousands who celebrated a Jewish holiday, attended Catholic mass, or heard inspiring sermons in hundreds of Protestant churches. Add up that crowd and it would fill your local football stadium many times over. Yet there's hardly a word in the paper.

Religion News Is Big News

The year that our reporter combed the religion beat, he interviewed hundreds of pastors, rabbis, and laypeople representing dozens of denominations. He listened to dozens of sermons and heard everything from sacred classical church music to Hebrew chants to contemporary Christian pop music. He was stunned to find so much going on in a world of religion that most of our newsroom staff neither understood nor knew existed.

What about your newspaper? Is it covering these matters? Does it even have a religion editor or significant religion news features at least once a week? Does it address the key issues affecting religion today? Does it open its editorial pages for discussion of various viewpoints, especially those that differ from its own editorial policies? Does your rabbi, priest, or pastor know anyone at the newspaper?

Does your newspaper report the demographics of religion in your own area? What percentage believe in God? How many go to church, mass, or synagogue each week? Does it report the outreach programs sponsored by local congregations? What are they doing to help the needy in your inner cities, and how can you get involved? Who are the truly great religious teachers in your community and what are they saying?

Why the Press Distrusts Religion

My guess is that your answers to the above suggest that there's much work to be done. That explains, in part, the work of the First Amendment Center at Vanderbilt University, where relationships between religion and the news media have been studied in depth. What the university group found was revealing, though not surprising. Religionists and journalists distrust each other, while many clergy are convinced that news coverage is biased and unfairly negative. It went on to state that in the average newsroom there is probably more ignorance about religion than bias.

The Vanderbilt group ended its report with some constructive suggestions. The clergy need to better understand what's considered newsworthy, they need to provide the media with easier access, and they should sponsor programs that will help educate the media on complex religious issues. At the same time, the media need to take religion more seriously, they must add staff and increase coverage, and they must provide continuing education in areas of religion. All practical, on-target advice.

From my perspective, Vanderbilt's most important work had to do with a survey it conducted about newsroom attitudes toward religion. Frankly, there's been a flood of misinformation on the subject, and

> ## On the Record
>
> *My father was a young boy from Poland, and my mother a young girl from the Ukraine. Both fled religious persecution, both pursued economic opportunity and, though nothing came easy, they watched their children grow up in a land of economic opportunity, political liberty, and religious freedom.*
>
> *Freedom is a process in which we are all involved, non-stop. To the degree that through my broadcasting and writing I have been able to steer people in the direction of freedom, I am content.*
>
> MARVIN KALB
> Former television correspondent
> Public policy professor,
> Harvard University

much of it was laid to rest with this study, which found, among other things, that 72 percent of newspaper editors nationwide say religion is important to them. When asked what their religion was, only 4 percent said "none." That compares with 10 percent in most polls of the general public.

Too many of the most passionate members of the religious community think our newsrooms are loaded with a bunch of heathens, and that simply isn't right. I know from my years in the business that newsroom staffs care too. They're just as affected by the good and the bad in their communities as anyone else. What's important is that the amount of media coverage be in proportion to what's critical in the lives of the readers. If a newspaper consistently misses good stories that readers care about, it eventually loses circulation.

Encourage Faith Keepers

During my time at *The Herald* we worked hard to improve the situation. We invited dozens of religious leaders to the newspaper for open discussions about how we could do a better job. Their criticism of us was warranted in many cases, and we took their advice to heart. Over time, our religion coverage was tripled, with more stories going into the key local sections and with more about people who were doing important things in their houses of worship published in our zoned community coverage. We called the feature "Faithkeepers," and it became an assignment our young reporters sought out, principally because it was a fascinating beat and it gave them a chance to show off their talents.

At the same time, though, I was appalled at the ignorance of many clergypeople about the press in general. Most had never met a newspaper editor, and they had no desire to do so. The dialogue between newspapers and the religious community was almost nil. Keep in mind, too, that some of those who complain the loudest about the media are constantly arguing among themselves about ultimate truths. As a Presbyterian, I am often shocked and dismayed at how various Protestant denominations fight over doctrine. Sometimes the debates become very ugly and very un-Christian. And, from a newspaper editor's perspective, it's a very difficult and complex story to cover.

Mining the Riches of Faith

Why is faith so important? Because a key impetus to the renewal of our country's basic values centers on faith. Our country was founded by leaders who recognized a higher authority and created a constitution that protected individual belief. And our democratic values have been nurtured through our religious beliefs ever since.

Don't get me wrong. I do not include myself among those who would like to see a "Christianization" of America, even though I am unashamedly a Christian. In South Florida, I dealt daily with a complex cross section of race and religion: Christians and Jews, cynics and doubters, Muslims and Buddhists, and some who have no idea where they are. I always respect the rights of others to believe as they wish, or not to believe at all. However, those who differ from me have an equal responsibility to respect where I am coming from. In the end, it's impossible to compartmentalize our lives. We can't be one thing at church or in our homes and another at the office. Frankly, I believe one of the reasons for the impotence of faith in America is that so many who profess a certain religious belief do not live that belief in the real world. It's reserved only for their places of worship. That kind of faith will never invigorate a community or nation.

In my dealings with issues of religion in public, my greatest problems often came from some very narrow-minded, self-righteous crusaders who had no room for other viewpoints. Theirs was an exclusive club. Periodically, groups of church leaders would come into the newspaper to complain and they had absolutely no idea where I was coming from. You'd think from their comments that I was the worst human being on earth. Little did they know that religious faith and prayer were central to my life too.

Real faith enriches life. It does not restrict, nor does it exclude. I am not naive enough to think that everyone will believe as I do. But I am enough of an idealist to imagine a resurgence of interest in matters of faith and spirituality. We are missing out on so much when we confine ourselves to the here and now. I encourage you, if you have not already done so, to examine your heart, what you believe, from where you draw your inspiration.

As we transcend our daily lives and focus on higher truths, I am convinced we will find ways to make our world a better place in which to live and raise our children.

God wants you to make something special of your life. In the end, the thing that matters is what others see in us and, above all, what God sees in us.

Chapter 2

Meaning

Shaping Your Legacy

Meaning is not something you stumble across, like the answer to a riddle or the prize in a treasure hunt. Meaning is something you build into your life. You build it out of your own past, out of your affections and loyalties, out of the experience of humankind as it is passed on to you, out of your talent and understanding, out of the things you believe in, out of the things and people you love, out of the values for which you are willing to sacrifice something. The ingredients are there. You are the only one who can put them together into that unique pattern that will be your life. Let it be a life that has dignity and meaning for you.

JOHN GARDNER
Founder, Common Cause and Independent Sector

Faith Keeper

If you preach the gospel in all aspects with the exception of the issues which deal specifically with your time, you are not preaching the gospel at all.

MARTIN LUTHER

I went to college during the calm and conservative years of the mid-1950s when President Eisenhower provided fatherlike reassurance to a generation battered by depression and war. All we thought about was getting a job and settling down just as our parents had hoped we would. Then came the beat generation followed by the hippies with their existential philosophy that flaunted meaninglessness as a way of life. Today, curiously, we are recycling such thoughts with a new generation known as X. I fear that yesterday's teenagers examined our lives and concluded there was little meaning to be found. Success, yes. But little meaning.

If a youngster is watching you, would he see a life that really *meant* something?

The words from my friend John Gardner, now a professor at Stanford University, came from a speech that was later printed and distributed widely. Some fifteen years later, his comments were found in the wallet of a twenty-year-old woman who was killed in an auto accident. The search for meaning was apparently no idle quest for this young person. John's remarks gave her hope, affirming that meaning is not a rare commodity limited to class or position. It is elusive only to those who insist on looking beyond their own hearts, for I believe the Lord instills each one of us with both the desire and the ability to find meaning.

Using Your Faith to Set Life's Path

The ultimate meaning of life starts on the solid ground of faith in God. It is He who gives us meaning. It is the Lord who provides the blessings of life, the good things that we so often take for granted.

Is the meaning of your life centered on God? What is the bottom line of your life? How will you be remembered? Will you finish strong? Are you willing to make a new commitment to the Lord in your service to others?

Always remember that God is working through you and He has a mission for your life.

What Does Your Life Mean?

Perhaps the last time you thought about the meaning of your life was at a funeral. A close friend about your age dies and suddenly you find your-self wondering, "Wow, he was too young to die." And then a little panic sets in. Am I on track with my life? Where is it going? What does it mean?

Relax. There's no mystery in finding meaning in life. It's all around you. One of the things that has helped me in this department is to approach each day expecting to find at least one treasure to add to my storehouse of meaning: good music, the birth of a child, a walk on the beach, a spectacular sunset (even a mediocre sunset!), prayer and quiet reflection, discussions with good friends. When we begin to see the value inside each experience life gives us, even tough days can add meaning. Reflections on life's meaning can be caused by good experi-ences and bad, but we are usually too busy to give those experiences any thought. Remember, the ingredients for a meaningful life are all around you. It's what you do with them that counts.

Take, for example, money. If handled wisely and generously, it can add meaning to your life. I love the biblical story about the widow's mite. From her poverty, she still gave to others, and it enriched her life. The point of that story isn't that we should all be poor but that we should adopt a more carefree and generous attitude about the money we have. For too many, money becomes a priority—an end rather than a means. Instead of enriching your life, it enslaves you with greed.

Work is another area of life that can give you meaning, but it can also make you miserable. If most everything you do centers on work, you are likely to be a terrible parent or spouse. If not terrible, at least boring. Very boring. On the other hand, if you approach your work as a gift that is balanced with the other good gifts in your life, work—even on those days when nothing seems to go right—adds meaning to your life.

Running on Empty

One of the saddest realities of our culture today is the number of people whose lives are characterized by emptiness—literally and spiritually.

The nest is empty; the bank account is full; the promotions and plaques designate success and achievement. But somehow, all those good things aren't enough. If you fail to practice reflecting on what is meaningful and adjusting your life to those priorities, you are likely to wake up someday and find that nothing means anything anymore. Go to work. Pay your bills. Perform the perfunctory social obligations. Then start all over on Monday.

What about you? Who are you and what do you want to become? Why are you here? What does your life mean? What are your goals and dreams? Do you know what's really important in your life or do you feel yourself drifting?

Could you summarize the essential values of your life and, if so, are you living by them? Does what you do reflect the best in you? Could you recap the meaning of your life and carry it around in your wallet so that you could measure progress?

Set the book down for a second and write the answer to this question on a sheet of paper or on a blank page in the back of the book: What is it that gives your life meaning?

Was that a tough question for you? Too often, we set those questions aside

On the Record

When I look back over my life, and ask myself what is important, the first thing I think of are our children. If our children had not grown up to be caring, responsible, independent adults, I would have felt, whatever else I might have accomplished, I had failed in the most important responsibility God gives most of us the privilege of undertaking.

My Senate responsibilities involved long hours away from home throughout their growing-up years, but I tried to always be there when they had a game or school event that was important to them. Our times together as a family were very important to me as they were growing up, and we still enjoy doing things together.

SENATOR SAM NUNN
Democrat, Georgia

for some day when we will have time to think about them. But you know what? Unless you begin asking them now, you will never find the answers. And even if you do, what good will it do you later? Your life needs meaning now if you are to enrich your life and the lives of others.

In my years of newspapers and government service, I have found that most everyone wants to live a meaningful life. We want to be thought of for the substance of what we do, for our accomplishments, for our love of families, for our concern about others. We want to make a difference, but we sometimes forget that we're talking about a lifelong commitment, one that requires patience.

A Gift from God

Life's meaning doesn't come from "doing our own thing" without regard to the needs around us. Meaning is not something selfish people find very easily, nor in the end does it come from material things. Rather, the meaning of life ultimately is a gift from God to everyone. It cannot be bought, not even by those who equate money with power—and nothing else.

Meaningful lives shape legacies, and it is through legacies that we are remembered. To be remembered well is an essential endorsement of our character. We call it our reputation and it is priceless. Reputations take a lifetime to build, and only seconds to destroy. They reflect our family roots and the extent of our commitment to key personal values that we hope will rub off in positive ways on others.

The other day I read a newspaper story (I'm still a news junkie) about a policeman who was arrested for not only soliciting a prostitute but also stealing her money when he had finished using her. What a sad story. Here was a man who was married, had a family and a position of respect in his community, and he threw it all away. The mistake was not the actual indiscretion, but a life that had no moorings. He did not know who he was.

It takes strong personal conviction to know who you are, to know what you want to become. Then, even greater strength and commitment are required to orient your moral compass in a direction that will get you there. If you succeed in that effort, you will find the excitement of a life lived well and lived with meaning. I guarantee you that policeman would give anything to trade his current predicament for a stronger commitment to a meaningful life.

The journey of such a life always requires changes. In fact, it was out of a desire to build more meaning into our lives that my wife and I chose, after thirty years in the newspaper business, to return to California, which had been our home for many years. We wanted to devote more of our lives to serving others and to promoting those values we believed ultimately important in life. For you, it could be a change in career, learning a new skill, or "dialing down" your lifestyle so that you have more time and resources to devote to others. When we returned to the West Coast, Joan enrolled as a graduate student in a Southern California Presbyterian seminary. After an intensive series of courses in Theology, Hebrew and Ancient Greek, she has earned a master's degree in theology from Westminster Presbyterian Seminary. She is thriving on this personal "repotting." Why? Because it has sparked important new meaning for her life.

The point is, we need to avoid "coasting." Some refer to "getting in a rut." Whatever you may call it, I think you know what I mean. Can you be honest enough with yourself to examine where you are and determine if that's where you ought to be? And if you sense an emptiness within, will you take the necessary steps to refill your tank with meaning and new direction? Or do you really like living in that rut?

> ### On the Record
>
> *I have undying respect for the broad-shouldered family man and woman who care more about their kids than themselves, and they are willing to make sacrifices so that their children can succeed. They are what made this country go. They work hard, raising a family, taking risks and doing their very best.*
>
> FRANK BORMAN
> Former astronaut
> Las Cruces, New Mexico
>
> *I hope my children find something they passionately love to do. If so, they'll never work a day in their lives.*
>
> NANCY REYNOLDS
> Corporate director and former White House aide
> Santa Fe, New Mexico

The Press and Meaninglessness

One of the reasons so many people have difficulty finding meaning in their lives is that they often have a distorted view of life. And chief among the messengers of such distortion is my former profession. If all you did was read the front-page stories of most daily newspapers in this country, you might conclude that life is pretty rotten, so why bother.

As a newspaper publisher, I sometimes fought with my newsroom over what constitutes news. I believed fervently in maintaining the delicate balance between reporting what I call "hard truths" and uplifting news features. Newspapers, of course, have a sacred responsibility to pursue the truth, but they also have an equal obligation to celebrate the goodness of their communities. If all we report are the rapes and murders and stories of crooked businessmen and politicians, we are not telling the truth about our communities. Adding to the problem are shrill editorial opinions that divide people rather than inform them.

When I became publisher in late 1982, it became my urgent task to take *The Miami Herald* through one of its most tumultuous chapters. For a generation *The Herald* has been one of America's most respected newspapers, but it was losing ground. In less than twenty years, Miami had changed from a sleepy southern town to a dynamic, often divided, international city whose majority was Hispanic. South Florida had almost doubled in size and had shifted from a 20 percent Hispanic minority to a 52 percent majority, mostly Cubans who had fled Castro in search of freedom.

The impact of all this on our newspaper was enormous but, to a large extent, the newspaper had not changed with the market. The results were often disastrous. We had lost touch with too many readers and we weren't meeting the needs of our advertisers. It's never easy to change the culture and built-in attitudes of a huge institution, and *The Miami Herald* was no exception.

This is a major problem for many newspapers today. In recent years several thousand newspaper employees have been laid off and a few dailies have been closed. Editors and publishers alike are scrambling to fight rising costs, declining readership, and a reduced advertising base to support it all. In this environment, more attention must be given to what's on the minds of the American people.

For example, our country has become more conservative. We want to live within our means. We are looking for greater meaning in life, founded on moral conviction. The concern about fundamental values runs deep, and the media have been slow to catch up with this thinking. It's no wonder that much of the public perceives newspapers as being far too liberal, far too arrogant, and, seemingly, dedicated to Bad News. Sometimes newspapers are guilty on all counts. I predict that those newspapers that arrogantly push a liberal ideology on our generally conservative population will continue to lose ground and flounder.

On the other hand, newspapers that rediscover the power of good news—and there is plenty around to be reported—will prosper. Sometimes reporters and editors don't search hard enough for it. Most of it isn't seen as headline material. Some is fairly tedious and unglamorous, but it is real. There's a revolution going on out there, and it's based on values and morality. It's big news and it isn't making the consistent, day-to-day headlines as it should.

> ### On the Record
>
> *My accomplishments center on being the father of three terrific children, helping create a wonderful family that is close-knit, loving, and reflective of the right values. I just want to be remembered for doing the best I could for my family and for my colleagues at Knight Ridder.*
>
> JIM BATTEN
> Former Chairman and CEO,
> Knight Ridder, Inc.

Wes Gallagher, the highly regarded, no-nonsense, former general manager of the Associated Press, put it this way: "The average reader is earning a decent wage, has a satisfactory family life, is proud of his children and of what he has accomplished. He also is proud of his country. He has come to feel that somehow what he reads is threatening his way of life and he resents it."

To deal with this valid criticism of the press, Al Neuharth, the controversial founder of *USA Today*, has called for a new journalism of hope, one that "chronicles fairly the good and the bad, and leaves readers fully informed to judge what deserves their attention and/or support."

I believe that good things happen in life because they are driven by a spirit of optimism and enthusiasm and that newspapers play a crucial role in fostering that spirit. Positive attitudes do make a difference, even when—in fact, especially when—life has dealt a cruel hand and the options seem impossible. Those who are optimistic generally find greater meaning for their lives. But if all we read in our newspapers and see on the evening news are stories of things gone wrong, who can blame the next generation for adopting often nihilistic and meaningless outlooks? Who can blame any of us for becoming cynical?

Miami Nice?

One of the biggest lessons I learned during my years in Miami is that a key to finding meaning in life—and in helping others find meaning— is to honor the good that is around us. At *The Herald* I wrote a weekly Sunday column in which I found dozens of opportunities to celebrate ordinary people who I felt were doing extraordinary things to reflect important values. In the process, these good people were showing the rest of the world what true meaning is. During the Thanksgiving and Christmas seasons, we published a "Holiday Wish Book" highlighting human need in the community. The feature generated hundreds of thousands of dollars in donations for the needy. Each year, the newspaper gave awards to outstanding high-school seniors who served their community. We honored chief executives who excelled in business, and we sponsored The Spirit of Excellence program to help celebrate those who were making South Florida a better place in which to live.

All this was done in the belief that honoring good people makes for good communities. And good communities, in turn, help create an environment conducive to meaningful lives.

Miami reflected the best in life, and the worst. In that context, we were no different from any other city in America today. Some crises there, however, were quite severe. The contrast was often incredible— from the five Pulitzer Prizes for journalistic excellence we won during my years as publisher to five devastating riots resulting in some fifty deaths.

Adding to Miami's crises was the flood of crack cocaine that poured into the country from Colombia and elsewhere in South America. Our neighborhoods became battlegrounds in the war against drugs. Cocaine cowboys shot at each other in parking lots at the malls while Colombian warlords worked feverishly to meet the demand for drugs. No one was safe from the crisis: in the last year we lived in Miami, my family and I experienced two attempted break-ins and an armed robbery, all in the privacy of our own home.

God's Work

So why did we stay for thirteen years? The people. I have always found it fascinating that in cities with severe problems, there seems to be an unlimited supply of caring people. On the other hand, when life is too comfortable, people tend to be selfish. We witnessed this so often in South Florida where the problems of crime, drugs, and hurricanes were real and seemingly endless. When we pulled together to solve the latest crisis, we all tended to find greater meaning and significance to what we were doing.

When facing community controversies, I found enormous help in 2 Corinthians 5:20:

> God uses us to persuade men and women to drop their differences and enter into God's work of making things right between them (The Message).

South Florida is no different than any other urban center. Today, all cities struggle to reduce crime, balance budgets, create jobs, and improve education. Many of these problems defy solution but I am confident we can find answers. Frankly, we have no choice.

On the Record

If everyone could have had my mother, we wouldn't need a police force today. She was strict in a very calm way.

I valued my relationships with literally thousands of shipmates and civilian friends at all levels scattered worldwide. That friendship was based on mutual respect and trust, as well as concern for others.

ADMIRAL THOMAS MOORER
Former Chairman of the Joint Chiefs of Staff

Your questions "What three accomplishments do you consider to be the most important in your life?" and "What three values would you like to be remembered for?" are better answered by others who may have occasion to review my life.

WILLIAM REHNQUIST
Chief Justice
Supreme Court of the United States

In times of controversy and crisis, I learned that meaning in life requires one very important principle: maintain a steady course. Let your life be determined by core values that never waiver and make your important decisions from that perspective: where you work, who you marry, where you worship, and where your kids go to school. And don't worry about criticism. There were times when I was attacked for being too conservative and too liberal—all in the same day!

Can a Nation Find Meaning?

If you listen carefully to those who are running for office, you will hear a nation in search of meaning. People ask: Where is America's soul? Why can't we live within our means? Why is our government such a failure? Why can't we be safe in our own neighborhoods? What about family unity, personal values, and religious faith? Can't anyone be trusted anymore? Where is our country's sense of decency?

No narrow advocacy group or political party can claim credit for this shift in public attitude. This deep concern transcends partisan politics, ethnic diversity, and religious denominations. Rebuilding America's moral fabric is not just a Republican cause; it's one for liberals and independents too. This is not a just-arrived, soon-to-pass fad reflecting the results of one election.

Public anger has been building for years. Study opinion polls. Go hear a sermon at your church or synagogue. Talk to any of the hundreds of state and local politicians who have been thrown out of office or forced to retire in the past two or three years alone. Listen to radio talk-show rhetoric or the debates in Congress. Sound out your neighbors. Speak with young people. Read newspaper editorials and news-magazine cover stories. Look at the best-seller list in your local bookstore.

Perhaps their comments and occasional outrage can serve as reminders that you are not alone in the fight to restore fundamental values of life. In fact, you are in very good company. On the front lines are those who struggle to make ends meet. They care about their country, and they work hard to do the best possible for their families and friends.

These dedicated Americans seem never to make headlines, nor do they seek them. Their incomes are modest but they turn in a good day's work—every single day. Above all, they believe in the importance of personal example. They know they cannot expect good values from others unless they reflect them in their own lives first. They care about their own reputations and are driven by a strong desire to do the right thing. Their lives have meaning, and if they are given a voice in their communities, this country will rise above its current malaise.

Of course, the United States has problems. Some are maddening and a few seem to defy solution. Somehow, though, we'll find answers. We almost always do. In our country, crises come and go with the pendulum swinging from the best of democracy to the worst. Our heritage and our freedoms are all fragile, and so to survive, they must be nurtured, defended, reinforced, and protected by each of us.

For almost 225 years, the United States has reflected incredible resiliency, with an unparalleled record of self-renewal. At the core is an overriding belief that we can build a better future, one constructed with a spirit of enthusiasm and hope. But it will take a brand-new outlook on life from all of us.

God's Light

Helen Keller was once asked what she would do if she had three days to see. Her answer was a powerful testimony to finding life's meaning:

Faith Keeper

On the first day I would want to see the people whose kindness and companionship have made my life worth living. I would call in my friends and look for a long time into their faces. I would also look into the face of a new baby. I would like to see the many books which have been read to me.

The next day I would get up early to see the dawn. I would visit a museum to learn of man's upward progress in the making of things. I would go to an art museum to probe the human souls by studying paintings and sculpture.

The third morning I would again greet the dawn, eager to discover new beauties in nature. I would spend this last day in the haunts of persons where they work. I would stand at a busy street corner, trying hard to understand something of the daily lives of persons by looking into their faces and reading what is written there.

On the last evening I would go to the theater and see a hilariously funny play, so as to appreciate the overtones of humor in the human spirit. Yes, by God's light in Christ, seeing what matters and beholding the extraordinary in the commonplace.

If your life seems a little flat and you had difficulty answering the question, Where do I find meaning? You might spend the next three days as if they were the last days you could see.

Chapter 3

Authenticity

No Waffles, Please

There's harmony and inner peace to be found in following a moral compass that points in the same direction regardless of fashion or trend.

TED KOPPEL
ABC's *Nightline*

Faith Keeper

The older I become and the more I read and pray, the more I understand that there can be no real love or honesty without a real faith in God. There is no way I can overemphasize how important the gift of the Holy Spirit has been to me.

WILLIAM HOEVELER
U.S. District Judge
Miami, Florida

The bulletproof window in my seventh-floor office provided an almost unobstructed view of the heavily guarded main entrance to the American embassy in Madrid. Outside the gate, about two hundred Spanish and Cuban demonstrators were shouting pro-Castro and anti-American slogans. To them, I was a "Yankee imperialist" and a "tool" for the exiled Cuban community in Miami.

I had barely unpacked my bags as the newly appointed U.S. Ambassador to Spain and already I was wrapped in controversy. After thirteen years in volatile Miami, I suddenly felt right at home in Madrid. As publisher of *The Herald*, I was used to protests. I had had my fill of boycotts, bomb threats, massive riots, and a never-ending war against drugs. Now I had been attacked by both extremes—the passionate anti-Castro Cubans in South Florida and the naive pro-Castro sympathizers in Madrid.

It was ironic that the embassy protesters in Madrid were attacking me for my anti-Castro comments. For fifteen years my *Miami Herald* colleagues and I had been accused of being Castro sympathizers. I must have been doing things just about right because now I had angered both sides on an issue that has plagued the United States for thirty-five years.

Over the years I've learned that the best way to ruin a night's sleep is to waffle your way around a tough call. Wimp out on the big decisions and you'll be miserable, but take a stand for what you believe and you'll have that inner peace and confidence that allow you to face anything with grace. Sure, you won't win the popularity contests, but in the final analysis you will be respected as an authentic person. What this nation needs is more authentic people.

"To thine own self be true" is more than a memorable phrase from Shakespeare. It's an absolute if you want to finish strong in everything that you do. To try to please everyone is disastrous. You'll hate yourself for it, and you'll lose whatever respect and dignity you have with others. For me, this unexpected controversy in Madrid was no time to waffle.

The demonstrators had marched to the American embassy to protest remarks I had made about Fidel Castro in a wide-ranging interview published by *ABC*, one of Spain's leading daily newspapers. I wanted to remind Spain how hypocritical it was that the Communist dictator was coming to Spain for a conference of Latin American leaders who were there as symbols of extended democracy in their region.

The issue of Cuba and Castro is hot in Miami and, as I learned, equally passionate in Madrid. But I knew where I stood and said so. Being a diplomat doesn't mean you give up your core beliefs just to please people. Castro had been a disaster to his own country, and on occasion, some leaders from the Cuban American community had gone overboard in their efforts to force support for their cause. On one occasion, for example, a local radio commentator had his legs blown off by a car bomb simply because a few anti-Castroites didn't like his moderate views.

Though new to the job in Madrid, I was in familiar territory as I watched the protest that day. Mercifully, demonstrations in Spain are carefully controlled. For example, it is illegal to protest without a police permit and those applying for one must cite the purpose, location, number of demonstrators to be involved, and precise time frame for the protest. If any of the approved ground rules are violated, protesters are hauled off to jail. Those with a cause get to state their case, and then they must quietly fade away.

Not a bad system, I thought to myself.

From the very beginning of the historic Madrid summit, the Gray Beard in wrinkled army fatigues was out of place. This was a man who had made a mockery of human rights, throwing thousands of political enemies in prison without recourse and murdering thousands of others. Even the consummate diplomat King Juan Carlos could not temper his comments, which were seen as a stinging indictment of Castro during the Madrid summit. Freedom in Latin America was inevitable and Castro could not escape His Majesty's message. As the meetings progressed, the Cuban leader became more and more annoyed.

In a further twist of irony, the diplomatic corps was seated near the delegation of Latin leaders during the opening ceremony of the Summer Olympics in Barcelona. In the middle of the group was Fidel Castro. I did everything possible to avoid anything even close to a chance encounter with the Cuban dictator. What a field day my Miami critics would have had with a page-one newspaper photo of Castro and Capen! I would have needed bodyguards in Miami too.

When the conference ended, Castro flew to Santiago de Compostela, the capital of Galicia, a lush region in northwest Spain that appears much like parts of Ireland. After a brief visit to his father's birthplace, Castro insulted his host, Manuel Fraga, a longtime Castro friend and president of Galicia, and immediately cut short the remainder of his trip.

In the middle of the night, the leader of Cuba woke up and demanded that the Spaniards turn on the runway lights so that he could leave immediately. Local government officials were summoned from bed and rushed to the Santiago de Compostela airport where, at 3:00 A.M., Castro took off for Havana. The Cuban leader had embarrassed and infuriated his friends in Spain. He also had pulled the rug out from under those loyalists who had so passionately defended him in front of the American embassy.

Castro was a loser at this Madrid gathering of Latin American leaders and it was my duty to say so. Easy words for an ambassador? No, but necessary ones.

On the Record

Without values, nations, societies, and individuals can pitch straight to hell.

Individually, we must develop compassion, a willingness to work, loyalty to family and friends and organizations, the courage to face temporary defeat and not lose forward motion.

JAMES MICHENER
Austin, Texas

My mother, a concerned, committed, and courageous schoolteacher, could not contemplate defeat for herself or permit goals short of excellence in her children.

EUGENE PATTERSON
Former editor, *Atlanta Constitution*
Former president and CEO, *St. Petersburg Times*
St. Petersburg, Florida

What If I Offend Someone?

In times of controversy, it often seems easier to duck the issues; to let little of your real views be known so as not to offend anyone. Whether it's a local school issue or a tough decision to make as a parent, the path of least resistance is often the one chosen because we think everyone will end up feeling good. And yet, I have always found serenity in knowing that my life is driven by certain values and principles that never change. You can too. No amount of shouting or personal attacks can take away the key anchors of your life if you know what you believe and stick to it. That's what being authentic is all about.

One reason our country is in so much trouble these days is because too many of us have refused to stand up for those values we believe in so passionately. We have worked so hard to understand the other person that we have failed to help him or her even to consider the principles that drive our own lives. I'm not suggesting you ignore others or trample insensitively on their views, but you are entitled to your ideas too.

A Spanish Blessing

In Spain, Joan and I did a lot of things to show the country that America cared. In Spanish, the ambassador and his wife are referred to as *los embajadores*, suggesting a team. We liked that inference. But not everything we did pleased everyone. At the embassy, for example, Joan started each meal with a blessing, whether we were alone in our small, private dining room on the second floor or seated with seventy-five others in the formal first-floor dining room where we entertained hundreds of guests each month. As we bowed our heads around the table, we held hands as was our custom at home. This tradition was a shock to many Spaniards, especially the men, who tend to be very macho in their dealings with others. We wanted to be authentic, and prayer was a very important part of our authenticity.

Soon the word leaked out and *Tiempo*, one of Spain's leading weekly newsmagazines, ran a feature story about our tradition. The article was headlined "The Praying Ambassador." The editors were outraged, accusing me of trying to remake Spain, whose socialist leanings on issues of divorce and abortion had driven gigantic wedges between the government and the church. Our simple effort to thank God for His many blessings was seen as an attempt to reunite church and state. Today, that magazine article is framed in my California office—as a badge of honor. Spain seems to have survived its Protestant "praying ambassador," and I enjoy the peace that comes from being true to my beliefs.

Squeezing the Orange Bowl

Soon after I became publisher, our newspaper took on the venerable Orange Bowl Committee for blatant discrimination. Some of the committee's practices were relics of the old South. For example, committee membership didn't begin to reflect Miami's diversity. In reality, it was a rather closed organization. I know because I was one of them, having been elected a year earlier. But if I was to remain true to my beliefs, I had to use both the weight of *The Herald* and my spot on the committee to fight for change. I wasn't about to quit the committee, however, because I have always believed in working from within to make changes. Most times, complaining from the sidelines accomplishes very little.

The Orange Bowl group also had unrealistic standards for selecting high-school bands for its nationally televised parade on New Year's Eve. The result: local, predominantly black, high-school bands were prevented from participating because their uniforms and training were not up to par. It was basically legal discrimination because nothing was being done to give these kids a break. It was shameful.

As a further measure of insensitivity, the group had a long tradition of honoring the college teams selected to compete in the Orange Bowl classic at private clubs that discriminated. Here, where no black members were allowed, the committee would entertain teams whose majorities in most cases were black. It was the ultimate in hypocrisy. *The Miami Herald* took on the committee, and I took the heat. But we did it because it was the right thing to do, and I insisted we do it because my own personal integrity was at stake.

Later, changes were made and the Orange Bowl Committee, having lost much of its own authenticity, has earned it back. And some people in Miami are still mad at me over the whole thing.

Do you work for a company that discriminates against minorities in similar subtle, "legal" ways? Are you troubled by your church's plans to abandon the city and move to the suburbs? Does your school showcase its athletic program at the expense of academics? These are all tough—and very common—issues that need people like you to take a stand. If you do, you'll make your community better, and you'll regain your self-respect. But it won't be easy. It will seem as if you're a lone ranger, because there aren't many truly authentic people around these days.

Decision by Opinion Polls

Hardly anyone says what he or she really thinks anymore. If something's popular today, we're for it. If it's unpopular tomorrow, we change directions. We think of concession as the better part of valor and allow ourselves to make important decisions by testing the water first. Politics and politicians are the worst offenders. Polls become their anchor, even though it's a drifting one. They point their fingers into the wind, take the pulse of the latest poll, and bravely charge forward thinking they have sensed what the majority believes. Personally, I think that's pathetic.

Where are those willing to lead without regard to what's popular at the moment? Where are those who are willing to be courageous, even if it means they will lose the next election? Where are those with the determination to stand for something, and to be consistent and unwavering in doing so? In these troubling times, we need policies that are driven by unchanging principle, and we need leaders who are willing to maintain a steady course, simply because it's right.

Unfortunately, some of my media colleagues contribute to this public-opinion craze. Some sponsor their own polls and use them on a regular basis to decide which stories to follow and how much importance to give them in the newspaper. Sometimes, there is almost a herd mentality as reporters get sucked into the frenzy of the story. Have you ever wondered why both *Time* and *Newsweek* have identical cover stories so often? At best, polls can indicate trends, but it is dangerous and misleading to draw too many conclusions from any given survey. Often, the public is fickle and unpredictable, and relying heavily on polls draws us away from common sense and visionary leadership.

But don't be too hard on the politicians and the press. We all like to be on what seems to be the winning side, so we put our fingers to the wind and go with the flow. Just remember, the winning side isn't always the right side. Personal authenticity results from decisions based on key personal values such as honesty, courage, compassion, humility, and perseverance. Your credibility evolves based on what you do in life and the reputation you create along the way, not on whether everyone agrees with you. As time passes, your authenticity can grow, especially if those values underlying it are reflected on a consistent basis.

Without authenticity we are fakes and pretenders, lost souls wandering through life without direction. Friends are limited because we have not earned their respect.

> **On the Record**
>
> *In pardoning Richard Nixon, I did the right thing for our country. Sure, I paid a price but it is a price a president has to pay when he thinks he's doing the right thing, whatever the polls show.*
>
> FORMER PRESIDENT
> GERALD FORD
> Rancho Mirage, California
>
> *The average citizen wants his or her officials to use common sense for common good but often those voices are drowned out by the extremes in both parties who are usually wrong but never in doubt.*
>
> SENATOR SAM NUNN
> Democrat, Georgia

Families fall apart because there is no rock-solid base that enhances love and unity. We are ineffective at work because we are not trusted. Nothing seems to add up because we drift along, never quite knowing what we stand for or where we are headed.

If this sounds like you, maybe it's time to reevaluate what you believe and how that is reflected in the way you live.

Dick Enberg, the highly regarded sportscaster for NBC, tells a powerful story about authenticity, one that involves Wimbledon tennis, which he has covered since 1979. As tennis stars leave the locker room and head for center court, they must pass under a brass plaque that reminds the competitors of their need to be modest, whether they win or lose. Inspired by Rudyard Kipling in his poem *If,* the quote simply says this:

> *If you can meet triumph and disaster and*
> *treat those two imposters just the same. . . .*

As Dick Enberg told me, "No one represented that message better than Chris Evert. She never pouted in defeat, never gloated in victory." This outstanding woman was more than a superb athlete; she was an authentic one, too.

How to Be Real Again

Authenticity starts with family and close friends. Your love and respect for family and friends are nurtured by the very soul of your being, driven by values that count. In the end, these values will shape your legacy and mine. For you, it might mean getting in touch with your family again. Spending time with them—not just quality time, but real time doing the ordinary. It might mean canceling a business trip so that you can get together with some friends for an evening of fun and fellowship. So many people I meet are in such a hurry but reflect a shallowness that belies their busyness. You can't be very real if you're rushing through life.

No Apologies for Your Faith

Equally as important is your belief in something greater than yourself— a religious faith that acknowledges the reality of the Almighty. It's a shame that we have been led to think we must keep this part of our lives so private. I shouldn't have to apologize that I am a Christian, and you should never feel your own belief in God should be a secret. I believe all the evidence points to Someone special, beyond human understanding, who has created the incredible blessings of life and the world around us, however imperfect we might have made it.

That belief in something bigger than yourself gives your life a moral foundation that guides your behavior. You no longer face decisions with a need to be liked, but with a desire to be true to those core beliefs.

Religious people are often mistakenly called fanatics when, in reality, they are simply people who refuse to bend with public opinion. How many times have you heard someone say, "I don't agree with him, but I respect him because I always know where he's coming from"? Isn't that how you want to be remembered?

Most of us have a general idea about what makes our lives authentic, but often those priorities are not in clear focus. So, it's a useful exercise to draft your own statement of values. Write them down, refine them, and then put the list aside for further reflection. Share the list with your family or a close friend. Their input and candor can help. As you share your list with family members, here's a scary question that will be enormously helpful: Do I live these values? Listen to their answers and you will learn where you need to adjust your lifestyle.

> ## On the Record
>
> *One of my most important accomplishments was getting my good friend and colleague, Jerry Ford, accepted and confirmed as vice president over the objection of President Nixon.*
>
> *Jerry was the right man at the time. It would not have happened had I not been counselor to the president and in the White House at the time.*
>
> MEL LAIRD
> Senior Counselor, *Reader's Digest*
> Former Secretary of Defense

This process of focusing on priorities can be the most important thing you do, because it will define who you are now and who you intend to be. If your actions don't match your words, you are in trouble. If you are indecisive and unfocused, chances are you don't really know what you believe or what's important to you. Regrettably, the world is full of people like that. They live out their years drifting along with a selfish perspective that often turns to misery in old age. By then, it's too late to rediscover who they want to be.

Putting your thoughts on paper is a powerful way of identifying key points and of keeping score. Perhaps that's why that young woman carried John Gardner's comments in her wallet. I'm not talking here about a passing thought on New Year's Eve. Those resolutions are usually a dime a dozen, and usually are forgotten the very next day. I'm talking about commitment—a promise to live your life in a way that will reflect all that you want to be. It starts with a few key values that define who you are.

Think about people you know. Most have led lives that can be encapsuled in a few words: He's a workaholic. She's very religious. That person's generous. Another is egotistical and selfish. Some put family first, while others cheat on their spouses. A few are known as cynics, while others seem cheerful all the time. Some care deeply about their religious faith; others worship their money. Some can be trusted with everything; others would cheat on almost anything. Some are smart but lazy; others survive on hard work.

What would people say about you? What do you want them to say?

One little tool that helps me think about my own personal sense of authenticity is a list of absolutes I call "headlines to live by." I'll be the first to confess I do not always live up to them, but I review them often to remind myself of the person I want to be.

Headlines to Live By

- Above all, cherish your family, friends, and faith in God.
- Stand up for what you believe. Life is not a popularity contest.
- Earn the trust of others. Everything in life starts with it.
- Be willing to take on new adventures. Don't torture yourself with what you might have done.
- Move forward decisively, and don't leave any of yourself on the shore.
- Do your best, no matter how modest the task. Be all you can be, every day. You never know who is looking up to you as a mentor.
- Be an encourager, especially to those without hope.
- Be optimistic in everything you do. Attitude is far more important than talent.
- Celebrate diversity. We are a nation of minorities, and will become more so.
- Serve others. The spirit of volunteerism is uniquely American and key to our future.
- No matter what chapter of life you're in, no matter what your

age, start strong and finish strong. Never tolerate half-baked efforts.

How about your own list of headlines? As you develop them, be absolutely honest about who you are and who you want to become. You must be candid about your strengths and weaknesses, your likes and dislikes. Because there will be distractions and unexpected hurdles along the way, you must be prepared to maintain a steady moral compass to guide you through life's highs and lows.

Don't Wait for Tomorrow

If you sense that your walk doesn't match your talk, you can change directions today. If you wait until tomorrow to set your priorities, you'll never do it. If you wait until you can get away to a mountain cabin for a few days, you'll get to that cabin and spend all your time skiing. It's human nature to put off the really critical things of life. It's chilling indeed for me to remember that eight leaders I respect and care deeply about participated in the research on values for this book but never lived to see the results. Sadly, they remind me of my responsibilities to make the most of each day.

So get out that pencil and start wrestling with these questions today: Who are you? How will you be remembered? What values are most important to you? Which ones will you pass along to your children and which ones will they accept because they have seen your inspiring commitment to them?

These are tough, tough questions, but they cannot be avoided. Your answers will define your authenticity. Drifting along with no goals or no purpose in life is a sure ticket to failure. You must decide who you are and what's most important to you. Vacillation and hesitation become "values" too. Lousy ones.

The Creator has given you a perfect blueprint for who you are. Only you can determine if you will turn that blueprint into an authentic picture. You are the only one who can lay out the route for an authentic life. Authenticity is not a final act for the sunset years but a pattern for each day along the way.

Chapter 4

Character

What Will Your Child Inherit?

Leaders can decide to be primarily concerned with leaving assets to their institutional heirs or they can go beyond that and capitalize on the opportunity to leave a legacy, a legacy that takes into account the more difficult, qualitative side of life, one which provides greater meaning, more challenge, and more joy in the lives of those who leaders enable.

MAX DEPREE
Leadership Is an Art

Faith Keeper

Remember that when you leave this earth, you can take with you nothing that you have received—fading symbols of honour, trappings of power—but only what you have given: a full heart enriched by honest service, love, sacrifice and courage.

FRANCIS OF ASSISI
circa 1220

When Bill Clinton ran successfully for president in 1992, he was dogged by questions about "the character issue." Because of allegations of marital infidelity, pundits questioned whether he was fit to lead our nation. It almost did him in, and it still haunts him.

Stop and think about that for a moment. It's the 1990s. Ethics are "situational." We're not supposed to "impose" our morals on anyone. And yet, everyone got all worked up about rumors of a candidate's philandering.

I think that's as it should be. It proves that regardless of how far we've come along in the spirit of free thinking and the relentless pursuit of pleasure, character matters. The American people don't want a president who did not honor the important vows he made to his wife, or to anyone else for that matter.

Character is that combination of virtues that gives us a legacy to leave for others. I learned just how important such a legacy can be on a recent trip to Auschwitz.

As my wife and two daughters walked with me through the iron gates of the concentration camp, I was reminded of a high-school classmate who had a string of numbers tattooed on his left arm. Miraculously, he had escaped Poland at the end of World War II after surviving the living hell of the Holocaust. His German captors had let him live, but the physical and emotional scars would remain forever. It was an ugly reminder of Hitler's determination to number every Jew, and then eliminate them all. Before this shameful chapter ended, the Nazis had murdered six million Jews, more than three million in Auschwitz alone.

Our trip to Poland was motivated by a desire to understand better what was in the hearts and souls of the Jewish community in South Florida. We had hundreds of Jewish friends in Miami, and we wanted, as tough as it was, to understand the horrors of their heritage. A year earlier, we had traveled to Israel with a group of Jewish and Christian leaders from Florida and had been deeply moved by the experience, highlighted by an emotional stop at Yad Vashem, Israel's national memorial to Holocaust victims.

After a five-hour bus ride from Warsaw, we arrived in Auschwitz, now a hauntingly quiet farming community. Today, the concentration camp there appears much as it was found in 1945 when Allied forces liberated the region. Wooden shelves where feeble Jews were stacked row upon row. Huge windowless gas chambers with the gas pipes still protruding from the ceilings. Open ovens where thousands of bodies had been cremated. Outside was a well-known stark brick wall where thousands were shot, a process eventually deemed too slow by German efficiency experts. Nearby were stacks of production efficiency reports and huge collections of glasses, human hair, and gold fillings that had been removed from victims and separated for recycling.

It was a chilling sight.

In 1940 Hitler rounded up all Jews in and near Warsaw and forced them to live in a small quarter of the city. To this day the area is known as the Jewish Ghetto. For three years, 400,000 Jews lived seven or more to a room, struggling every day against starvation, disease, and death. The Nazis had mandated that all Jews would wear white armbands bearing a blue Star of David and the label "Jude" (Jew).

Food was scarce and medical care was denied. Jewish-owned businesses were shut down, valuables and bank accounts were confiscated, and travel was restricted. Later, children were taken from their parents and husbands separated from their wives. Schools were closed, and thousands of Jews were rounded up each morning to be hauled off to unknown destinations. All lived on the edge of catastrophe, and disease was rampant. Some were executed on the spot for refusing Nazi orders. The brutality was beyond human understanding.

In this terrifying environment, millions of Jews all over Europe were forced to face up to some ultimate questions. They feared the worst, but no one could truly have anticipated the horrors of the Holocaust. Adolf Hitler's goal was to slaughter them all, and he almost succeeded.

In anticipation of their impending deaths, many began to put their thoughts on paper. There was nothing material to will their children, but they could do something far more important. They could pass along their personal values, their hopes, their agonies. They wanted, desperately, to capture their legacy in the event they did not survive the horrors of war. And so, in a cruel and terrifying setting, the Jews of Warsaw's ghetto wrote of love, of caring concerns for their children, of dreams for generations yet unborn. They called them ethical wills, reflecting a practice that dates back to Old Testament days when men gathered their children for advice, warning, and praise.

Though Hitler and his henchmen had murdered millions, he had failed to destroy their legacy. All material wealth was gone, but something far more important remained. The collection, safely stored in the concrete basement of the nearby synagogue, had miraculously survived relentless bombings that, in the end, leveled the entire city. And so, to this day, this rare collection of ethical wills has preserved the legacies of thousands of very brave people. Many of the documents are included in Rabbi Jack Reimer's excellent book, *Ethical Wills.* Here's a sampling of what a few contained:

On the Record

My father taught me to be results-oriented and never to give up. My mother taught me compassion, love, and patience.

J. W. (BILL) MARRIOTT, JR.
Chairman, Marriott Corporation
Bethesda, Maryland

My accomplishments start with family, and then forty-six years of public service and working to impact foreign policy in a variety of ways.

CONGRESSMAN
DANTE FASCELL
Democrat, Florida
Former chairman, House Foreign
Affairs Committee

> *You must go to work alongside people of other nations . . . and you will teach them that they must come to a brotherhood of nations and to a union of all nations with God.*
>
> YOUR MOTHER, 1940

> *My dear, fortunate sons. We sense the end is near. It will not be long before they finish us off. . . . Don't take foolish things to heart. Be happy, contented people; be good*

human beings and loyal sons of your oppressed nation.
Never abandon your land or your people. Fight for freedom
and social justice. Be just and honest.

SHULAMIT RABINOVICH
Kovno Ghetto, Poland, June 6, 1944
(Note: This mother wrote this on D-Day but did not live to celebrate
the victory.)

Fellow Jews. We lived, we loved each other, we fought, and
we believed in the God of Israel.

BERL TOMSHELSKI
Carved on the wall of the synagogue
Kovel, Poland, 1942

Your Ethical Will

What would happen if you knew you were going to die tomorrow?
Would you be satisfied with what you have accomplished so far? Would
you be proud of the values you are passing along? Does your family really know you? In short, is your legacy in shape?

In our culture today, we think of a will as a formal device for passing
along wealth. It usually is a financially oriented, legalistic document
only to be understood by lawyers who specialize in estate matters. Wills
have become a complicated tax-planning device loaded with incompre-
hensible language, Internal Revenue Service regulations, and cold business terms. For most, a will is an impersonal instrument focused on
money, taxes, and actions that will help avoid taxes.

But when you stop and think about it, there is nothing more important that you can leave for your loved ones than a rich legacy. A wholesome reputation. Values and beliefs that become gifts more priceless
than trust funds or heirlooms. Wills of the material and legal variety can
be contested, but your ethical will is indisputable.

What are *you* leaving for those who follow you?

One way to understand what will go into your ethical will is to think
about your own grandparents. How much do you know about them?
Can you recall their full names, their work, their education, their hob-

bies, their values? Are there certain character traits that you associate with them? Did you inherit any of those traits? If you can pass that test, move back only a few years to the next generation. Can you even name your great-grandparents? Do you know anything significant about them?

Now, reverse roles and move the clock forward a generation. What will your children and grandchildren know about you? And what will they filter down to their kids and grandchildren about you? Chances are, if you're optimistic, always finding the good in other people and circumstances, they will inherit that and pass it on to their children.

Do you begin to see how important your character is? In terms of the fate of any culture or society, is it somewhat daunting to think of what your role is in shaping the future?

> ## On the Record
>
> *My father taught me never to write off any human being—no matter how low he has fallen. Often my congregation asked me to be silent but my final decision was always dictated by my conscience. I could not sell my birthright for a mess of pottage.*
>
> RABBI IRVING LEHRMAN
> Temple Emanuel
> Miami Beach, Florida

Academy Award–winning movie producer Steven Spielberg may be known for any one of his films, but he's working on a legacy that is more far-reaching than his movies. He's devoting much of his time these days to capturing the history of the Holocaust on the Internet. Through the miracle of this new technology, he is leaving an important message for generations to come: "I want to teach our kids not to hate," Spielberg says. Thus far, he has recorded 100,000 hours of interviews with 50,000 of the estimated 250,000 survivors of the Holocaust. It is a massive undertaking. "It is easy to turn your back on history," the producer says. "But, we will not let that happen."

The ethical will you leave your family and friends may not be as extensive as Spielberg's Holocaust project, but it is no less important.

Everyone Has a Legacy

Like it or not, you *will* leave something behind. Unfortunately, sometimes what we leave is a legacy that contributes to the erosion of goodness. In

Miami, a well-known banker had built his reputation by running a huge financial institution and by giving generously to the community. While hundreds of families depended on the bank for work, many thousands of shareholders and depositors trusted the banker with their deposits and investments as shareholders. It turned out that the bank executive was a crook. He squandered the bank's funds; he used company assets for personal benefit, buying paintings, entertaining lavishly, and using bank funds to maintain his personal yacht. Before the binge was over, the bank collapsed, thousands had lost millions, and the banker is now in prison in shame.

Our newspaper also nailed corrupt judges who were receiving illegal endorsements from lawyers, police officers who were dealing in drugs, and a superintendent of schools who used tax dollars to install gold faucets in his home. We uncovered money-laundering scams, telephone solicitation rip-off artists, and lawyers and insurance people who were conspiring to defraud insurance companies and their policyholders.

I don't mean to imply that you may be a crooked businessman or that a jail term is just around the corner for you. But how do you handle the little things, like bringing home a towel from your motel room or letting your fourteen-year-old pass as a twelve-year-old to qualify for the children's menu? You see, those lapses of character stick. Those who look to you for guidance measure your words against your example.

Character in the Arena

In my opinion, trends in the ranks of college and professional sports do not bode well for the character development of our young people. I realize that most people involved in those arenas are decent, honest men and women with solid values. But because of the enormous visibility and influence of sports, even one lapse of character sends the wrong signals to impressionable youth.

When professional athletes are arrested for using drugs or beating up their girlfriends, they let down thousands of fans. When basketball stars push referees and pro tennis players shout at linesmen on close calls, they give terrible messages about the need to respect authority.

Often it was our duty at the newspaper to take on such abuses, and I can assure you we won no popularity contests for doing so. During my years in South Florida, the University of Miami was involved in one football scandal after another, and we ran major stories about most. For the coaches then involved—and for some blindly passionate alumni—winning seasons were more important than winning character. Tragically, similar patterns have occurred in other colleges that have allowed powerhouse football programs to get out of control.

When my older daughter was a student at Stanford, the university's administration was involved in several major scandals. It had flunked the course on character and, in the process, done serious damage to the school's reputation. Worse yet, those involved had set a terrible example for young people.

Such scandals are reminders of how quickly a life of good work, or an institution that has worked for generations to build a good reputation, can be undone by poor judgment, or worse.

It's important for all of us to speak out when we see something that is flagrantly wrong.

On the Record

I was a superb wife. I was an excellent mother and I'm a supportive, role-model grandmother.

And, I'd like to be remembered for my integrity, generosity, and for courage in the face of adversity.

ANN LANDERS
Chicago, Illinois

I would like to be remembered for my integrity, my fairness and hard work. I strive for uncommon excellence in all that I do, although it remains a distant goal.

TOM JOHNSON
President, CNN
Former publisher, *Los Angeles Times*

Consistency and Character

Character building is not something that can be inherited one generation and ignored the next. Nor is it something you build on weekends. It's not done by pretending, or when convenient. Character is the reflection of the whole person, founded in virtue and morality and lived constantly. Like a cyclist who automatically leans in the right direction to maintain balance, the person of good character knows intuitively how to speak the truth, care for others, and live meaningfully.

You can't be a devious leader in the office and a dedicated father at home. In the end, your vices catch up and your kids will be the first to discover such double standards.

The message is simple. Be clear in who you are, and share your character with those you love. If you do, the future generations of your family will know who you really were, and what virtues were central to your life. Those brave Jewish people in Warsaw left behind their character. Will you? Their souls will live on for generations. Will yours?

Chapter 5

Self-Esteem

You're the Best You've Got

God hath entrusted me with myself.
EPICTETUS

Faith Keeper

To do God's work is to do what is right when no one is looking . . . and doing what is right when everyone else is compromising.
CHARLES SWINDOLL

I once had a high-school teacher who gave me a wonderful gift: my first major dose of self-esteem. Several other students and I were struggling in our first year of algebra, but Mr. Manheimer convinced us we could tackle the subject. A superb teacher and encourager, he helped us through the year. We did so well that he kept our group together, and by graduation we had soared through algebra, geometry, and the equivalent of two years of college-level calculus. And all this was years before our school systems had designed advanced-placement programs. Wally Manheimer had created his own.

I never use calculus today; in fact, I defy anyone to describe clearly what calculus is. But that's not important. What mattered was the self-esteem this dedicated teacher had inspired in his students simply by making them feel good about themselves because they had climbed a very tough academic hill. Sadly, I never had a chance to thank Wally Manheimer for his wonderful gift, but my guess is that like most teachers, he knew in his heart what he had accomplished. In the end, that is all that matters.

Because of his gift, Mr. Manheimer gave us the ability to transfer our confidence into other aspects of our lives, thus making us more successful there too.

To feel good about yourself and to know in your heart that with hard work and determination you can get the job done are important personal values in a very demanding world. It's called believing in yourself, and to do so creates self-esteem.

Start Strong to Finish Strong

In our home, we believed that the first step for our children to start strong in life involved nurturing self-esteem. I am convinced that enhancing your children's self-esteem is one of the greatest contributions you can make to their lives. We tried to build it in a variety of ways, including one that our children will never forget.

As soon as our kids could walk and talk, we taught them that the way to meet our adult friends was to look them in the eyes, smile broadly, shake hands firmly, and greet them in a voice the world could hear. There was no hiding out in the upstairs bedrooms, and no wimpy words were allowed. At first, the requirement was greeted with groans and a sense of panic, but as time went by, they accepted it all as the price of room and board.

In 1969 these Capen Marching Orders were put to the test. On a cold, snowy afternoon in January, my family and some fifty senior civilian and military leaders had gathered in the Pentagon for my swearing in as a deputy assistant secretary of defense.

With two of our children looking on (our third was born four years later), Secretary of Defense Mel Laird, my new boss, administered the oath of office while I placed my left hand on the family Bible held by my wife, Joan. Our very young kids stood nearby.

New civilian appointees in Laird's Pentagon were honored with this very special swearing-in ceremony conducted in the secretary's huge office in the presence of his key civilian team and top military. Most of my assistant-secretary colleagues were there that day, along with a dozen senior military commanders, starting with the Joint Chiefs of Staff and the secretaries of the Army, Navy, and Air Force. At the time our son, Chris, was three and his sister, Kelly, eighteen months. They were too young to be intimidated by all the military brass but old enough to know the rules. They performed like a couple of Marine Corps drill sergeants that day. Well, almost. Chris stood respectfully at my side, while Kelly sat impishly on the floor in front of three generals and an admiral. This small demonstration of independent thinking, for which our daughter is well known to this day, clearly was a first for the four-star brass.

Quickly bored by the whole thing, she discovered, to her absolute delight and fascination, the 120-button telephone panel behind Mel Laird's desk. The system gave the defense secretary instantaneous access to the president and most major commanders around the world. Somehow, we had failed to anticipate the need to tell our kids that the secretary's hot lines were off limits. Mercifully, Kelly never knew that the rows of phone buttons could be activated only when the phone was off the hook, so we avoided World War III that day.

The point of this humorous episode is that had I jumped all over Kelly for her independent spirit, I would have carved a bit of her self-esteem out of her. She would have felt there was something dreadfully wrong with her for having the normal curiosity of a youngster. I often wonder how many little spirits we crush when we deny kids the right to be themselves.

Building on Success . . . and Failure

Do you remember when you were a kid how good it felt if Mom or Dad praised you for something you did all by yourself? It made you feel great, didn't it? If you were as lucky as I was, you had ample doses of those pats on the back, and it inspired you to always try your very best. That's what self-esteem does. It gives you a short-term "feel-good" reward, but more important, it sets a pattern for success, which is an ongoing reward.

> ### On the Record
>
> *It is crucial to find someone with high moral character to become your mentor early in life. When recruiting players, we choose character over raw ability. Reputation is important in our unique work environment where team members must work in harmony if they are to reach their individual potential.*
>
> JERRY RICHARDSON
> Owner of the Carolina Panthers

Surviving the Pentagon ceremony that day added a little self-esteem to our children's inventory, and that's the best way to start with *your* children: build on success. Riding a bike for the first time. Getting an A in a course. Winning a baseball game. Remembering to make their bed before school. Drawing a picture or building a model. These types of events offer natural occasions to praise your child and in the process build self-esteem. One success begets another, and the collection of achievements begins to shape self-esteem.

When it comes to helping your child develop a healthy sense of self-esteem, I have always believed that there are five critically important gifts that parents should pass along to their children:

- The anchor of a caring family and faith in the Lord.
- The power of as much education as they are willing to work for.

- The reassurance of unconditional love from their parents.
- Encouragement along the way, especially when times are tough.
- Self-confidence that creates self-esteem.

But what do you do when your child doesn't bring home a straight-A report card? In fact, he's never gotten an A in his life? Some kids will never hit a home run, never win a blue ribbon for a painting, never even make the JV team. How do you build self-esteem when your children aren't winners?

Thinking about winning is part of the problem, because self-esteem isn't about winning. My first efforts at math produced a lot of mistakes, but Mr. Manheimer never let me think I was stupid because I didn't do well. His praise for my efforts kept my motivation high. Too many times, parents are quick to jump on the mistakes their kids make, missing a great chance to praise them for their efforts, to remind them they are valued. If you want to see what I'm talking about, go to a children's-level baseball game and watch the parents. You'll see the dad who berates his child when she strikes out and you'll also see another dad who comes over and gives his daughter a hug when *she* strikes out. Now which girl is going to go on and be successful in baseball—or even in other areas of her life?

Never tie self-esteem too closely to success. Look for every occasion to catch your kids doing something right and praise them. Even when they fail, focus on the effort and rebuild their sagging feelings by reminding them that they always have another chance, and that you'll always love them no matter what.

There's great comfort in knowing who you are, and having a quiet reassurance of self-esteem. People armed with such confidence are better prepared to live life fully. They maximize the use of their talents and energy. They don't waste time worrying about what they might have done or how they failed. We all miss the mark. We all occasionally wish we had taken that other turn in life that is no longer an option.

Is Your Home an Oasis?

Most of us adults forget how mean kids can be, but it's a tough world out there for your kids. Talk about man's inhumanity to man. It's nothing compared to kids' inhumanity to kids. If your poor child happens to be the one who doesn't wear the "right" brand of sneakers, he's in for a very tough year. And if he or she has any kind of physical imperfection—from pimples to protruding ears—he or she will be mercilessly teased to such an extent that it can scar him or her for life.

That's why your home and your job as parents are so important. Think of your home as an oasis—a place where your children are safe from taunts and put-downs that destroy self-esteem. I know it's not always possible for a parent to be home when the kids return from school, but if at all possible, be there. Sometimes just a hug or listening to them blow off a little steam is all they need to keep their self-esteem intact. *They* know they are okay, even after taking some teasing, but they might need to test you a little bit just to make sure they are still loved.

> ### On the Record
>
> *Richard Nixon gave me sage counsel about the Office of the Vice President. He said I should stick with my strongly held views and never change to satisfy the critics.*
>
> *Another mentor for me is George Bush. He is one of the most caring individuals I ever met. He has a sense of decency and good manners, traits that I have tried to pass on to my children.*
>
> FORMER VICE PRESIDENT
> DAN QUAYLE
> Indianapolis, Indiana

Does this mean you should never contradict or discipline your child? Just talk to the Capen kids and you'll discover what a joke that line of thinking is. I'm a firm believer in a parent's responsibility to discipline children, but discipline should never be dished out in a way that tears down a child's confidence. I've always appreciated this bit of biblical wisdom for parenting: a soft answer turns away wrath, but grievous words stir up anger.

Be careful with the words and tone of voice you use when you discipline your children. Avoid terms like "You always" or "You never," and *never* resort to sarcasm or name-calling. As much as possible, follow any necessary discipline or criticism with a reminder that you love them. I know it can be tough sometimes, and like me, you'll make mistakes.

When you do, be a good example by apologizing.

Remember, most of us act as others perceive us to be. If a teacher says you aren't good in math, you probably never will be. If you believe you can't spell, you'll probably be a lousy speller for the rest of your life. If a coach tears you down, you'll probably never make the team. If the boss shows little confidence in your ability, you're not likely to hold the job. Some people are slow learners. Others fail several times before they get the hang of it, and then they move on to enormous success. To write off anyone—at any age—is a crime.

You May Be Better than You Think

Sometimes we have difficulty building self-esteem in our kids because our own sense of self-worth isn't all that great. Too many of us are far too pessimistic in sizing up our abilities in life. And if we're not down on ourselves, you can be certain others will be. We put a negative twist on ourselves. We focus on our failures (who *doesn't* have them?) rather than on our successes. And then we wonder why our kids can't look an adult straight in the eye?

Why not imagine yourself to be successful? Why not tell yourself—over and over again if necessary—that you can achieve, that you can win, that you are perfect for the job? So much of self-esteem is found in attitude. Like Hans and Franz on the old *Saturday Night Live* used to say, "We're here to pump you up!" Pump yourself up every morning. Tell yourself you will give your best no matter what. Forgive yourself ahead of time for the mistakes you *will* make. Then go out and have some fun!

During the Vietnam War, one long-term POW in Hanoi spent month after month of solitary confinement reliving memories and dreaming about the home he'd always wanted to build. He had no pencil or paper, only the expanse of his mind and memory. So in his head he designed his dream house, room by room, elevation by elevation, rendering by rendering. When he returned home, he recalled it all in full detail, specification by specification. Every dimension, every fixture, every beam—all designed and ready to go. Not one line on paper.

If the opportunity for you to succeed is not immediately at hand, dream about success. Let your mind wander along the road of things you'd really like to do.

What About Failure?

I hate the word *failure*, but I don't deny it happens. In the newspaper business, we had a chance to fail every day in nine editions and two languages. It drove me crazy when we made mistakes, especially the kind that involved printing retractions or making apologies. But I learned early in life that failure is inevitable. We don't have to like it, but we don't have to yield to its destructive powers either.

Frankly, I think a lot of Americans are dealing with personal failures. If we can trust the statistics, a good share of Americans have seen their marriages fall apart. Talk about a sense of failure. Add to that the growing number of white-collar men and women who have lost their jobs, the increase in personal bankruptcy filings, and . . . well you get the picture. It's easy to make a mistake and begin to think you're the only one who failed at something. Relax—you're in good company. It's what you do about it that makes a difference.

> **On the Record**
>
> *My brother taught me brotherhood, companionship, and unqualified love. My wife taught me self-worth and a sense of class.*
>
> GEORGE WACKENHUT
> Founder and CEO, Wackenhut Corporation
> Palm Beach, Florida
>
> *My mother taught me to do my best always and to never give up. My father taught me, by example, to want nothing else from any man, to work hard, to earn what you get, and to treat everybody fairly.*
>
> HUGH MCCOLL
> Chairman, NationsBank
> Charlotte, North Carolina

When life has dealt you a bad hand, go back and list the good things that have happened in your life. Recall your personal victories. Rank your blessings. Count your friends. Take joy in your memories. Inventory your successes in business or career. And, pray. Pray often. Pray as if your life depended on it. The spark that builds and restores self-confidence starts from within.

I take comfort from stories of people like John Grisham, whose first novel was rejected by many publishers. Maybe you need to remind yourself that often the people you admire most have experienced tremendous failure at various points in their lives. Those stories keep me going when I stumble.

Above all, be encouraged by the potential of your future. Don't ever put yourself or your feelings in the hands of those who are determined to drag you down. You have total power to control how you react to the criticism of others. Never let the cynics get under your skin. Be like the old Timex watches: takes a licking but keeps on ticking!

With your spouse, determine not to let conflict shatter each other's self-esteem. Every marriage has its challenges and disagreements. Even after thirty-six years of a solid marriage, my wife and I have occasionally, shall we say, failed to see eye-to-eye. To deal with those we have two rules: talk out our differences, and never go to sleep at night angry at each other. It may make for a few late nights of working things out, but you'll finally fall asleep at peace with each other, ready to greet the new day as a team.

Time for a Spiritual Faith-lift

Years ago Dr. Maxwell Maltz, a plastic surgeon, wrote an excellent book (*Psycho-Cybernetics*) about how he had given spiritual face-lifts to hundreds of patients whose egos had been badly battered by negative attitudes and low self-esteem. Through corrective surgery, he was able to mend horribly deformed physical appearances. But often, serious psychological trauma remained.

His patients had a hard time dealing with the attractive, new life his surgery had given them. It was tough for them to believe that others no longer should be shocked at their appearance because this talented medical specialist had miraculously reconstructed their faces. That's where the physician's positive attitude served to fortify the power of optimism in the new appearance and outlook he had given his patients.

With superb surgical skills, Dr. Maltz had repaired the outward appearances of his patients, but their self-esteem had not kept pace. "To the degree that we allow ourselves to suffer anxiety, fear, self-condemnation and self-hate," Dr. Maltz writes, "we literally choke off the life force available to us and turn our back upon the gift which our Creator has made. We have become far too pessimistic regarding man and his potentiality for both change and greatness."

Sometimes we overcome a problem but refuse to let that victory boost our confidence. We pass it off as a lucky break, or, with a false sense of humility, we convince ourselves that it was nothing. Like Dr. Maltz's patients, we got used to being ugly. This is why it is so important to celebrate your successes, no matter how small they might seem to you. Be kind to yourself. If you've struggled to lose weight, for example, don't wait until you shed twenty pounds to celebrate. Make every pound you lose a reason to pat yourself on the back.

Dr. Maltz called it a spiritual face-lift, but I'd like to think of it as more of a *faith*-lift. After all, faith is all about believing, and what we really need is the permission to believe in ourselves. Here's where my own personal faith is so helpful in giving me self-esteem, because I truly believe that I was created by God and that He did a great job on all of us. This allows me to start from a point of faith and great expectations, and fall back on that when things don't always work out for me.

Really Bad News

"Okay, Capen," you might be thinking. "Easy for you to say, but what about the real tragedies of life? How can I still hold my head up after losing so much?"

I am thankful for the great blessings in life I have been given. And though it hasn't been easy, I realize I have not had to face the kinds of tragedies that usually devastate a person. But I *have* observed a lot of tragedies, and what I've discovered is that even a father who loses everything he owns to a hurricane or a mother whose son is gunned down in a drive-by shooting can emerge with a strong sense of personal worth. In fact, it is often from their stories that my own self-confidence is given a boost.

Take the tragic story of Christopher Reeve. This talented actor who played Superman had everything that makes you feel pretty good about yourself: good looks, near-perfect health, fame, and family. Then, in a horse-jumping accident in 1995, his life changed dramatically. Now he breathes with the help of a respirator that allows him to speak in partial sentences as he exhales. Barely able to move his neck from side to side, he steers his wheelchair by blowing into a rigid plastic straw. Inspired by the unselfish love of his wife, Reeve has refused to feel sorry for himself, though it certainly would be understandable why he might.

"You begin to see," Reeve said in a TV network news special, "there is a future with the love and support of family, friends, and people. You also discover that your body is not you, that the mind and spirit take over." Reeve sees potential and opportunities he never dreamed he had. His positive attitude has protected his self-esteem. Not even a terrible, paralyzing accident could deter his ability to believe in himself.

I don't fully understand how this happens, but I've seen it so many times that I know it's true: even in tragedy, you have control over the way you see yourself. You can become bitter and feel sorry for yourself, or you can accept what has happened and be proud of yourself. To survive, no matter what the trauma, you must learn always to hope. You learn to adjust and make the best of the circumstances. There's no room to ask what might have been or to feel sorry for yourself. Christopher Reeve never did. He had a strong sense of who he was, and he wasn't about to let a terribly battered body destroy that belief.

Of course, Christopher Reeve can't do it alone, especially now that he is paralyzed. He has a great teammate in his wife, and self-esteem requires lots of teamwork.

The small Hopi Indian tribe in northern Arizona celebrates life, weather, and good crops with dances and the tradition of *kachina*, Hopi statues that represent important values. One of those little statues, named Tehabi, depicts a blind man carrying a small cripple on his back. Loosely translated, Tehabi means "I'll be your legs, you be my eyes." In honor of this Hopi message, my son, Chris, named his specialty publishing company Tehabi Books, a reminder that their business is driven by teamwork. So is self-esteem.

I see a similar thing happening within the African American community. Because of ongoing racism and the resulting economic disadvantages, most blacks have every reason to give up. A lot have, especially black males. But an amazing thing began with the 1995 Million Man March on Washington, and continued later with subsequent demonstrations supporting the essential role of dads. While initiated by the controversial Nation of Islam leader Louis Farrakhan, the event quickly became a forum for several hundred thousand fathers and sons who were showing their commitment to family and a desire to take charge of their own lives. The gathering was a message of reconciliation. But the real effect of the march was to lift up the image of black men *among themselves!* Young black kids from all over America had a wonderful reason to be proud and hopeful. Their fathers and friends had given them the precious gift of self-esteem. Upon returning to their homes and neighborhoods, many of these men have taken the ideals of the march to an even higher level. I firmly believe that as American black men begin to view themselves as successes, we will see a renaissance of black businesses, black culture, and black families contributing to the richness of our nation.

History is full of examples where entire nations have been nursed back to political health through strong leadership that helped restore self-esteem. Franklin Roosevelt did just that during the Depression. So did Ronald Reagan, who used his abilities as a great communicator to give Americans reasons to feel proud of their country.

Self-esteem is a potent engine that can inspire miracles in life. Through this resilience of human spirit, America has prospered longer than any other nation in history. No matter how scared we are, no matter how far down we may have fallen, we have an awesome ability to come back. I believe we can do it, and it has nothing to do with who gets elected or what bills get passed.

It has everything to do with what we believe about ourselves.

Chapter 6

Excellence

Reach for the Stars

The power of excellence is overwhelming. It is always in demand and nobody cares about its color.

GENERAL DANIEL "CHAPPIE" JAMES, U S A F

Faith Keeper

If the firm does not have a moral reference point, it has the potential to contribute to the bankruptcy of the human soul.

We have all been created in God's image, and the results of our leadership will be measured beyond the workplace. The story will be told in the changed lives of people.

BILL POLLARD
Former chairman and CEO, ServiceMaster

When I was a kid, my mother pounded into my soul the idea that anything worth doing at all is worth doing well. During my know-it-all teenage years, I did everything possible to resist her advice but, by my mid-twenties, I came to appreciate the wisdom of her words. Life's purpose is to do the best we can with what we have.

That's why I have carried the remarks of my good friend Chappie James everywhere I have worked in the past two decades. He was a powerful inspiration in my life. As America's first black four-star general, Chappie was an outspoken patriot who believed, above all, in the power of excellence. No one worked harder to overcome barriers, and no one did a better job of encouraging others to do the same. "Don't stop to argue with the ignoramus on the street who calls you a nigger," Chappie once said. "You don't have time. Pass on. Excel. Excel."

My friends and I will never forget the evening in San Diego when we honored Chappie at a dinner in our home. We had asked him to say grace, and he responded by singing his favorite Negro spiritual learned from his mother while growing up in a small house along a dirt road on the other side of the tracks in Pensacola, Florida. Chappie was the youngest of seventeen children.

Over and over again, his mother had pounded one simple message into his soul: people will reach out to help because excellence is a standard throughout the world and no one questions its color. "Remember, you are an American, not an African," she would say.

Chappie and I worked closely at the Pentagon on the prisoner-of-war issue during the Vietnam War. For three years, we crisscrossed the country speaking about the POW/MIA problem, demanding humane treatment for POW's, and giving hope to thousands of families who had lost loved ones in the war. Appropriately, he was one of the first to greet the men when they were released in Hanoi in 1973. Sadly, Chappie died of a heart attack in 1973 only a few weeks after he retired from the Air Force, but his powerful legacy remains.

While there were many dimensions to the life of this inspiring American serviceman, the one I remember best centers on excellence. I can still hear him shouting at his audiences, "Excel! Excel! Excel." A huge man weighing 260 pounds and standing six-feet-three-inches tall, he would hold the crowd in the palm of his hand. They loved the magic words of this revered black leader who, as he delighted in saying, never climbed into his jet fighter; he strapped it on.

That Winning Attitude

If you believe it is going to be a lousy day, it will be. If you think you are going to fail, you will. If you are convinced you can't handle your job, you are likely to lose it. If you are certain you cannot repair a relationship, you won't. It's all a matter of the standards you set for yourself. Most people accept far less than they deserve.

In the cauldron of newspaper publishing and international diplomacy, I had some ground rules to guide me.

- View your work as an example of excellence rather than simply a job.
- Never settle for mediocre performance, whether it is as a parent, a worker, or a community leader.
- Take time to learn from your mistakes.
- Try to improve in small, doable steps rather than trying to hit a home run all the time.
- Forgive yourself when you fail. There's always tomorrow.
- Teach excellence. Sharing lofty goals with others inspires the best in others—and in you.

The commitment to give any important task your best effort involves knowing that you can be a winner, and that a cheerful approach inevitably increases your chances of success. Such an attitude will also provide what you need to enjoy the God-given blessings of each day. And that too is a key value to live by.

Throughout my adult life, I have been blessed with responsibilities that stretched my energies and experiences. I was forced to do my best. Anything else would have been unacceptable to me, or to those who put their trust in me. My assignments in government and in the newspaper business were never easy, but I have worked hard under the principle that anything worth doing at all is worth doing well.

At *The Miami Herald*, we worked hard to publish good newspapers every day. Lee Hills, a former chief executive of Knight Ridder, Inc., the newspaper's parent company, had set the standard for all of us to follow. Among the most respected journalists of his generation, Lee had been a mentor to many in the business. In my survey, I asked him what values would outlive him. His answers explained why Knight Ridder's newspapers became among the nation's best under Lee Hills's editorial direction:

My Newspaper Beliefs

- Don't confuse entertainment with news, fact with fiction, reporting with advocacy, or media with journalism.
- Be sensitive. Do not go out of your way to hurt or embarrass people unnecessarily.
- Get it right, especially direct quotes. Get all sides. Don't cut corners.
- Be thorough, authoritative.
- Try to make your paper essential to readers.
- Provide services and information that help people with their daily lives, and make your paper a positive force in the community.
- I don't like "gotcha" reporting. Confrontational interviewing may be good TV show business and help ratings (profits), but it often distorts the news.

These principles defined the road map of our search for excellence at *The Herald*. Lee Hills reminded me of something Harry Belafonte said

On the Record

I learned from my father (who barely made it financially) the value of absolute integrity and the steady insistence on racial tolerance decades before this was an acceptable attitude in a small southern community. My mother quietly encouraged the need for a life of service beyond self-satisfaction.

TERRY SANFORD
Former governor and
U.S. senator (Democrat)
Past president, Duke University
Chapel Hill, North Carolina

after a concert while reflecting on his life and music career: "I have always tried to do my best with the very best." That's how we always felt in the presence of Lee Hills.

In the newspaper business, publishers often must deal with what I called "impossibilities." These were problems that defied solutions, ones that seem typical of cities such as Miami that have no majority and are deeply divided. To find consensus is truly an impossibility. Some neighborhoods (Little Haiti, Little Havana, Little Nicaragua, the Jewish community in Miami Beach, for example) have their own dialects, culture, and food. A few conducted their own foreign policy. Each fought for its own rights, its own perspective, sometimes without regard for the rights of others. Controversies and conflict were inevitable, especially with the newspaper that somehow must cut across it all.

During my stewardship, the newspaper uncovered corrupt county managers, judges who accepted bribes, a presidential candidate (former U.S. senator Gary Hart) who cheated on his wife, police who doubled as drug dealers, bankers who ripped off shareholders. Careers were ruined. People went to prison.

Initially, many investigative stories were vehemently denied, and the newspaper was attacked as an irresponsible villain. We always stood our ground because each story was carefully checked and we had confidence in our news staff. Inevitably, subsequent details would later validate our stories and justice would prevail.

One day I would be called a naive liberal, the next an uncompromising conservative. One day I was offering encouragement to the Castro regime, the next I was pandering to the Cuban American community. One day the newspaper was the only hope for the community, the next it was the sole obstacle to its progress. It would have been impossible to think that anyone would agree with our opinions or news stories every day. Not even my wife and closest friends did that.

It was often said that *The Miami Herald* was seldom loved but usually respected. We could ask for no more. While we were proud of our Pulitzer Prizes, I was much more concerned about the "prizes" we sought to earn from our readers. Excellence often means taking criticism for unpopular stands, and believe me, we took some pretty stiff criticism from time to time.

Excellence and Goal Setting

Excellence doesn't just happen. You will never achieve it if you don't aim specifically for it. That's why setting measurable goals is so important in the pursuit of excellence. It's not possible to succeed unless we do so.

Too often we drift along, indecisive and unclear about what we want most out of life. We mix the important with the trivial, and become frustrated because we have allowed minutiae to control us. And then we look back, too late, only to discover that we worried too much and accomplished too little. To excel in life requires a clear focus and a well-defined set of goals.

I like (and highly recommend) Stephen Covey's approach to excellence, especially as it relates to the way we manage our time. He refers to the "urgent and unimportant" and the "not urgent and important." Most of us spend our time on last-minute crises, but Covey advises us to try to spend more time in planning and preparation so that we don't have as many crises and so that we have more control over our destinies. We do our sloppiest work on those unimportant tasks that were left for the last minute. Planning is a key to excellence.

You simply cannot expect to program very much excellence into your life if you do not take the time to envision what excellence would look like. Take time to plan. Set goals. Reflect on your progress. Then rearrange your goals accordingly. This may seem elementary to some, but if you don't use some type of pocket planner to lay out each day's objectives and if you do not have a list of goals that you consult regularly, you should.

Goal setting involves both the big picture and the immediate. Bob

Buford, author of the book *Halftime,* recommends that you try to describe what your life would look like if it really turned out well. What do you need to do to reach that goal? You might need to make a list of those steps you need to take and review it once a week to keep you focused on a more excellent pathway.

People who excel never give up, and they never rest on their laurels. They take pleasure in each accomplishment, and they learn from their mistakes. When they fail, they pick up the pieces and move on to succeed again. Their goal is doing their best, and excelling along the way. I have always believed that when you approach personal goals with this passion, you are far more likely to attain success in all that you do. One success begets another. Each job well done provides new levels of self-confidence and motivation to move forward with even greater confidence, building one success on top of another.

I got a firsthand look at an elite group of people striving for excellence at the 1992 Summer Olympic Games in Barcelona. Thousands of athletes from around the world showed up in Spain, but only a small percentage would earn medals. Do you think that deterred them from trying? You wouldn't have thought so if you saw any of the performances. It was one of the most awesome displays of "want to" I have ever witnessed. The International Olympic Creed says it best: *"The most important thing in the Olympic Games is not to win but to take part, just as the most important thing in life is not the triumph but the struggle. The essential thing is not to have conquered but to have fought well."*

Olympic Egos

Speaking of the Olympics, I'm sure you remember the so-called Dream Team—the U.S. men's basketball team composed of NBA superstars. In my opinion, this was a case where excellent ability was not matched by spirit and attitude. I probably was one of only a few people that year who was very critical of the team, even though they walked off with the gold in Barcelona. Frankly, I was embarrassed by the group's arrogance. They arrived on a chartered jet and refused to stay in the Olympic Village where all the other athletes, including the prince of Spain who was on his country's team, were housed. The Dream Team had to be coerced into walking into the stadium with the other athletes during the opening ceremony. In competition, they made a mockery of the game. Sure, they were the best and could wipe out the competition, but they did so with a certain arrogance that I found obnoxious.

Achieving excellence, and knowing you have done so, requires humility mixed with grace. The American basketball team had little sensitivity about the thousands who had worked years to prepare for the games, only to lose in the first round. Sure, these guys were probably the best basketball players in the world, and I know their skill came from years of practice too. But along the way, they forgot who they were and began believing their press clippings. They could have been tremendous ambassadors for their sport and their country, but they blew it. The Dream Team did not bring glory to the United States.

On the Record

Courage:
Readiness to accept risk and take the lead when others doubt.

Commitment:
Decisiveness in choosing the right course and the endurance in holding to it.

Concern:
For the needs of others and willingness to sacrifice self-interest in their service.

EUGENE PATTERSON
Former president and CEO,
St. Petersburg Times

On the other hand, Great Britain's Derek Redmond became my hero, and he didn't even finish his race. A sure bet to win the gold in the 400-meter running competition, Derek got off to a superb start, moved out well ahead but, just short of the finish line, collapsed, screaming in pain. He had ruptured his Achilles tendon some fifty yards from what would have been certain victory in front of the royal reviewing stand where the diplomatic corps was seated. But that's not the end of the story.

Out of the stands jumped Derek's father and lifetime encourager. He lifted his injured son off the ground, put the athlete's arm around his shoulder, and dragged his son across the finish line. Derek Redmond had finished strong that day. His excellence was defined in terms of raw courage and determination—along with a dose of humility in letting someone help him when he was down.

You Don't Have to Be a Star to Shine

With all this talk about the Olympics and superachievers, you might conclude that excellence is available only to the elite. But excellence is an attitude, not a gift. Some athletes are naturally gifted but never achieve excellence. What should be encouraging to all of us is that more often, substandard athletes achieve way beyond their potential because they have caught the spirit of excellence—of never settling for anything but their best effort. Consequently, we find excellence in all walks of life: the carpenter who takes pride in the house he is building, the high-school lineman who opens holes for the running backs, a stay-at-home mom who reads to her kids at night despite her fatigue, the spelling-bee champ *and* the child who came in third, the Eagle Scout as well as the Tenderfoot.

It's the high-school student with the worst record for the mile but who tackles his next race with gusto, even though he knows he'll finish in last place. It's the young college coed who will never win a fraternity beauty contest but who has ultimate beauty because of her personality and determination.

The desire to excel inspires the mother who raises four children without losing enthusiasm for the uniqueness of each. It drives the fifty-year-old banker who has been merged out of his career—and finds a new one. It gives hope to the eighty-year-old widow who has picked up a new hobby or the terminally ill cancer patient who approaches each day with enthusiasm, curiosity, and gratitude.

To pursue excellence in life is a choice you make. Not every plan you set or every opportunity you choose will lead to success, but don't forget that success is never final. Nor is failure.

To excel can be a lonely experience too. Some are too lazy to do their best. Others don't have the patience to do so. Still others view excellence with envy. Admiral Hyman Rickover, whom I occasionally saw during my years in the Pentagon, was often outspoken on the subject of excellence. "For the person who strives to excel," the admiral said, "to shoulder responsibility and to speak out, there is an enemy everywhere he turns. . . . To struggle against these enemies and against apathy and mediocrity, is to find purpose to life."

The Excellent Journey

I have misled you if you think excellence is yet another goal that you reach after a lot of hard work. It is that, of course, but it is more. It is a way of life, a commitment to the ideal. You may never achieve your goal of being the best, but that does not deny you of excellence. At the same time, you may achieve certain high standards in life but not have the attitude of excellence. Your goals become the end rather than a means to a higher, nobler goal: to live a life of excellence.

For over forty years, I have been a subscriber to *National Geographic* magazine. Everything this group touches projects a commitment to reflect the best. Today, *National Geographic* is sent to 9.2 million members who have enjoyed the monthly and some three hundred books published in forty languages around the world. "Commitment to excellence and a sense of mission have inspired our staffers," says the group's CEO, Gilbert Grosvenor, whose grandfather founded the Society in 1890. Appalled by general ignorance about basic geography in our country, Gil Grosvenor invested $85 million in a ten-year program that has trained 150,000 teachers who have helped more than six million kids better understand geography. Gilbert Grosvenor and his staffers produce a stellar magazine because all they do is infused with an attitude of excellence.

On the Record

I would want to be remembered first for being a good family man and for raising five children in an environment that emphasized family values.

DON SHULA
Miami Dolphins
Miami, Florida

It is important for everyone to know where the lines are drawn. If you (the employee) find a situation where you must make ethical compromises to win, walk away. Our company wants only honest money.

THOMAS PHILLIPS
Former chairman and CEO,
Raytheon Company
Lexington, Massachusetts

When I was a kid, no one had ever run the mile in less than four minutes. Thousands had tried but all failed. Roger Bannister, now a surgeon in Great Britain, was one of those athletes. He had run hundreds of races but could never break that magical barrier. Then, on a chilly afternoon in May 1954 on a track in Oxford, England, Bannister became the first man to run the mile in under four minutes. Six months later, he quit competition to pursue his studies in medical school. Setting a world record was not the overarching goal of his life. Being the very best person he could be led him to approach every challenge with the spirit of excellence. (Ironically, a month after Bannister's world-famous race, an Australian athlete broke the Bannister record. Today, hundreds of runners have finished the distance in under four minutes. The message is clear: excellence is always a temporary condition.)

Set your sights high, then reach just a bit further. Make this "reach" your attitude toward life. Soon, you will see how the spirit of excellence invades your whole outlook on life. After all, if anything is worth doing at all, it's worth doing well.

Chapter 7

Trustworthiness

Can I Bank on Your Words?

The reality is, if we tell the truth,
we only have to tell the truth once.
If you lie, you have to keep lying forever.
RABBI WAYNE DOSICK
Golden Rules

Faith Keeper

Take a little time today to mend a
*   broken heart*
Or gather up the pieces of a dream
*   that's torn apart.*
Take a little time today to graciously
*   extend*
An outstretched hand to someone
*   who really needs a friend.*
Take a little time today to make a
*   life worthwhile*
For a stranger who can use an
*   understanding smile.*
Reach for heaven and reflect the
*   sunshine from above.*
Take a little time today to radiate
*   God's love.*

RAY MATHEWS

Few stories during my years as publisher of *The Miami Herald* caused more controversy than the one in May 1987 where we revealed that former Colorado senator Gary Hart had spent most of a weekend in Washington with an attractive young woman from South Florida.

A candidate for president of the United States, Hart was caught, red-handed, cheating on his wife. In an earlier effort to kill persistent rumors that he was a womanizer, Hart had denied it all and challenged the press to follow him. Weeks later, our newspaper received several tips that Hart would rendezvous with his friend in Washington.

The Hart story began with an anonymous tip passed along to one of *The Herald's* most talented staffers. The senator flatly denied the report, and blasted our editors for sloppy reporting. In following Hart to his new townhouse apartment in the Washington suburbs, we had generated considerable controversy and Hart was attempting to stonewall it all.

Basically, we had reported that Hart "spent the weekend" with an attractive young woman, but if we simply had said most of the weekend, our story would have been more accurate and Hart would have had extreme difficulty challenging our coverage. Nevertheless, our editors stood behind the essential elements of the story, and I backed them all the way, defending their work on national television and in press interviews.

Two days after the initial reporting, a weekly tabloid published a picture of the young woman sitting on Hart's lap in the Bahamas during an earlier fling aboard the yacht appropriately named *Monkey Business*, and the senator's ball game was over. Our published reports proved correct. Having lied to the American public, Hart was forced to reverse his story and his political aspirations crashed in flames.

The real story here was not about sex. I'm convinced that most people would have forgiven the senator had he admitted from the beginning that he was having an affair. What killed Hart's chances of future political success was his breach of trust. Americans desperately want to believe their leaders.

In the early days of the Hart story, some of my own colleagues chose to believe the senator and joined him in criticizing *The Herald's* performance. Many felt our reporters had improperly invaded the private life of a public figure. Both groups were wrong. Dead wrong. Syndicated columnist James Kilpatrick minced no words, summing it up this way: *"The Herald* received a tip, checked it out, found it reliable, and did what a great newspaper should do. *The Herald* exhibited good judgment and a high sense of responsibility. Hart exhibited neither one."

To this day, the debate continues about press rights and responsibilities in drawing the line between the public and private lives of public figures. In most circumstances, I would err on the side of privacy. In this instance, though, Gary Hart was not running for mayor of Aspen. He was seeking the most powerful office in the free world. In that high-stakes game, the slightest defect in character makes a difference. Here, truth counts, big time.

The public deserves to know as much as possible about those seeking to serve as president of the United States. What experience has the candidate had? Does he stand on principle, or is he likely to twist and turn with each passing fad? And above all, can he be trusted? No leader, whether in politics or in business, can survive long if not trusted.

Who *Can* You Trust?

One of the reasons for the decline of the American spirit is a pervasive loss of trust. Everywhere we look we find evidence that no one trusts anyone anymore. If you think I exaggerate, take a look at the ceiling or toward the corner of your local supermarket. Chances are you'll spot a security camera. We no longer seal marriage with a kiss. Instead, we sign prenuptial agreements, sometimes at the altar as part of the actual marriage ceremony. Banks delay clearing checks because they don't trust their customers. Hospitals refuse to accept patients because they are afraid they won't get paid. And our homes are secured with elaborate alarm systems because we're not sure we can trust the neighborhood security patrol.

Are we all really that dishonest?

Evidently we are. In the field of medicine, researchers at the University of Pittsburgh found that up to 20 percent of its doctor applicants for training fellowships lied about their research credentials. Moreover, 30 percent said they had published articles in journals that didn't exist. I'm not sure I want any of these people carving me up.

But doctors aren't the only culprits. *The Reader's Digest* once dropped 120 wallets, each containing fifty dollars in cash, on the streets of twelve large and small cities across the country. Its purpose was to test honesty in America. About 67 percent of the "lost" wallets were returned, indicating that, according to this unscientific measure, we are about 67 percent honest. Not a bad measure of trust either. How would you feel about someone who finds fifty dollars on the street and keeps it? How trustworthy would you think that person is?

Several years ago the Roper Organization surveyed the public about its perceptions of who's telling the truth. In this study, people said that the clergy told the truth 49 percent of the time, doctors 48 percent, their best friend 26 percent, the local newspaper 8 percent, the president of the United States 8 percent, and leaders of Congress 3 percent. What a terrible indictment of our system.

By the way, where would you rate yourself on truthfulness? What percentage of the time do *you* tell the truth?

Are White Lies So Little?

No one deliberately tries to be untrustworthy. Often, cheating begins in small, almost innocent ways. An exaggerated story. An excuse that simply isn't true. A padded expense account. An incomplete income tax return. Claiming sickness as a cover-up for taking the day off. We call them little white lies. Then the small ones grow into more serious violations of trust. We cut the corners by cheating on others and, in the end, we cheat ourselves. Why? Because trust is an ultimate value that protects an orderly, civilized society from chaos and anarchy. If there is no trust among neighbors, family members, and friends, nothing works.

Former Vietnam POW Harry Jenkins responded to my survey with an idea that is fast becoming archaic (see chapter 10): "My father taught me that a man's word is his bond." This simply meant that a person's word could be trusted. He didn't need to sign a contract or take an oath. If he said he would do it, you could consider it done.

Over the years, your own word takes on the strength of a "bond" or becomes porous and flimsy. For parents, this is an especially important issue. Most good parents want to do the right thing, but the danger is that they begin to promise more than they can deliver. Dad promises to take his kids to the movies but never does. Mom promises to help with the homework but there's never enough time. When you make those promises, you don't think you are lying, but your kids do.

True story: Two kids about ten years old were talking. One said, "Your dad's a liar." The other couldn't believe it: "What do you mean?" The first kid responded, "He said he was going to take us fishing some-day but he never has."

Ouch! I'm sure Dad really wants to take the boys fishing, but it might have been better not to say anything about it until the poles were loaded in the car. Once kids think you tell lies, they won't believe anything you say.

We do this to each other all the time: "Hi, Dick. Nice to see you. We've got to have lunch one of these days." After about the third time of that, you realize he didn't really mean it. Then you begin to wonder, When does he mean what he says and when is he just blowing smoke?

Newspapers and Trust

Trust is absolutely essential in everything we do—trust in marriage, between friends, at work, in public life. And yes, there is a trust rela-tionship between you and your newspaper. The ultimate role of the press is to seek the truth and, through it, to build trust. That's a tough task, and only a free and unfettered press can even hope to do it. Getting to the bottom of messy matters is often messy business. For certain, it doesn't win popularity contests for the newspaper business.

During the 1992 campaign, the media did a poor job of delving into Bill Clinton's record as governor of Arkansas. Matters of character and past conduct are very relevant, as we learned in the Hart case. What were Clinton's character values earlier in life? How did he make decisions as governor of Arkansas and who were his key advisers? Was he a person of conviction, or did he blow with the wind?

Paul Greenberg, the highly respected Pulitzer Prize–winning editor of the *Arkansas Gazette,* wrote often about Governor Bill Clinton's history of compromise, waffling, and indecision. The pattern was well known locally but seldom mentioned in the 1992 media campaign coverage. Regrettably, some serious charges involving illegal campaign finances and conflicts of interest were treated warily during the campaign by both the print and the electronic media. As a result, troubling questions have haunted the Clinton administration (including Hillary) ever since. Would America have voted differently? Probably not, but at least it would have gone into the adventure with its eyes wide open. Meanwhile, questions about honesty and trust linger, and that's unfair to the American public. It's unfair to the White House as well.

These are not matters of privacy. The answers to such tough but pertinent questions give the public clues about their leaders. Do they have the courage of their convictions or do they blow with the wind? Where do they stand on issues of family and religious faith? Can they make tough decisions and stick to them? How careful are they in selecting key advisers? How well do they handle stress?

The bottom line: can we trust those we entrust as leaders?

The rigors of the presidential campaign cycle every four years are

> ### On the Record
>
> *It appears possible that a permanent culture change has occurred at the Ford Motor Company emphasizing the importance of people and empowering them. If this should happen, it will be my greatest accomplishment in my professional life.*
>
> DONALD PETERSEN
> Former chairman and CEO,
> Ford Motor Company
>
> *Moving in a world of perceptions and images where almost everything or everyone is for sale, I have made sure that the characteristics of ethics, integrity, and honesty are key to my behavior.*
>
> MARIA ELENA TORANO
> Business Executive
> Miami, Florida

designed to smoke out important issues. Some people felt the press was too hard on Pat Buchanan after he turned in a strong showing in the New Hampshire primary in 1996. But it was that kind of scrutiny that flushed out some Buchanan staffers who were aligned with unsavory organizations. Trust of our leaders starts by knowing our leaders, and it's the job of the press to look beyond the phony campaign press releases, photo opportunities, and slick television commercials. We need to know how a candidate thinks, what his or her qualifications are, and especially what his or her core values are.

At every level, the public is demanding honesty, judgment, and integrity. Most Americans today think our country is in a dramatic battle to restore the nation's soul. In this environment, they are likely to judge their leaders and their key institutions, including the media, by a higher standard. If a candidate for the highest office in the land chooses to cheat on his wife, the public deserves to know. If that candidate compounds his sins by lying about them, the public deserves to know that too. Then, they can arrive at their own conclusion.

Each year *The Miami Herald* receives hundreds of news tips from readers and others across the country because the newspaper's reputation for pursuing violations of public trust is well known. State and local judges have accepted campaign kickbacks. County building inspectors have been bribed by contractors, and local cops intercepted huge caches of drugs and money, skimming off tens of thousands for themselves. A city manager wasted public funds, and a banker spent millions to fix up his home using customer deposits and shareholder earnings. *The Herald* scorched them all.

No matter how hard we tried, some people will never be convinced that the press has their interests in mind. Truth must prevail, regardless of the consequences, and it's the task of newspapers to report it. Newspapers are voices of the people and defenders of their interests. It's all part of the system of checks and balances built into our Constitution.

Don't get me wrong. Newspapers don't always live up to their own high ideals of truth and trust. Over the years, I have been involved in many circumstances where the media have not spread themselves with glory in earning public trust. *The Herald* could spend years building trust in the minds of its readers and have it all wiped out by a single unfair news story full of errors. That's why we worked so hard to earn the trust and respect of our subscribers and advertisers every day. I described it as our sacred responsibility.

But newspapers can often seem arrogant and self-serving. We sometimes hide behind the First Amendment when we really shouldn't. Former *Washington Post* editor Ben Bradlee did my profession no favor when, in his recently released book, *A Good Life*, he bragged, "I found it easier to cope with Washington by assuming no one ever told the complete truth." With such arrogance, it's no wonder the public sometimes doesn't trust the press.

There is a widespread sense out there that newspapers print far too much bad news. I got that message the hard and painful way—by facing reader outrage eyeball-to-eyeball. Believing that *The Herald* suffered from some of these same feelings of public outrage, I took our editors out into the community to meet the public. In the course of two years, we had over fifty sessions, with some attracting five hundred or more people. Using full-page newspaper ads, we encouraged the public to attend these town hall–type sessions.

We held meetings in Little Haiti and Little Havana. We met in a synagogue in Miami Beach and at an agricultural research center on the edge of the Everglades. Some readers came armed with huge files of old clippings and editorials. Some were irate, most had strong opinions, and a few just came along for the entertainment. We needed to earn their trust, and to do so, they deserved to know more about their newspaper and the people who ran it. Some complained about articles that had been published twenty years earlier. I had enough trouble defending what was happening on my watch, much less that of my predecessors.

At one meeting, held in a huge retirement community's auditorium, more than a thousand readers listened to our every word. They stayed more than three hours, with fifty or more lining up behind each of three microphones placed in the aisles. After it was over, one came up to compliment us for our bravery in putting up with it all and then told us that it was the best meeting the community had had since a local doctor spoke about sex after age sixty-five. Now, I thought, there's a trusting compliment.

The same comments came up, time after time. You make mistakes. We can't trust what we read. You are not fair. The reporting is slanted. You never get both sides of the story. There's too much rape, murder, and corruption on the front page. These were very tough words. Some hurt. Some were unfair, but most were on target. There were no excuses. We could do better.

We learned a lot through these public forums about how others felt about our newspaper, and I think we made some inroads in building better understanding about our goals and news policies. In response to what many had to say, we launched dozens of programs to restore their trust in us.

We expanded the story count on page one to allow a better mix of coverage, including some good news or at least a story good for a chuckle. We bent over backward to publish letters from readers, especially those who disagreed with our own editorial opinions. We also expanded sponsorship of important community events, launched awards for outstanding community service, and worked to bring onto our newspaper staff people who reflected the diversity of the communities we were serving.

We ran accuracy checks, calling people named in our coverage and asking them if our stories and headlines had been fair and accurate. We brought in hundreds of opinion makers for discussions on issues important to them so that we could do our jobs better. We added hundreds of personal profiles, many of them featuring ordinary people who were doing interesting things to make South Florida a better place. We expanded religion coverage, a subject grossly overlooked by most newspapers.

We did all this because we wanted to be trusted by our readers. We wanted them to be able to believe what we printed because it would make us a more valuable commodity. The same holds true on the personal level. You tend to appreciate more those you know you can trust. An individual cannot go to all the lengths we did to improve our position of trust in the community, but the principles hold true:

- Listen to advice.
- Do not repeat anything you know is untrue.
- Acknowledge when you make a mistake.
- Walk humbly (but don't carry a stick!).
- Make changes where necessary.
- Accept criticism as a friend.

On the Record

I want to be remembered for:

Willpower
> *To hang in there and grind it out.*

Faithfulness
> *To family with love and to cohorts with magnanimity.*

Judgment
> *Keeping myself and those whose reputations ride with me on a productive and relatively steady course.*

ADMIRAL JAMES
STOCKDALE
Senior American POW in Vietnam
Medal of Honor recipient

Little Things Count

I remember the time my daughter was pitching for her high-school team. It was an important game and her team was behind, but if the game went on much longer it would be called because of the two-hour time limit. At a crucial moment, her coach asked the umpire for time-out to talk to her pitcher. She wanted my daughter to slow down the game by taking more time on the mound. In this way, the game would be called, the score would be canceled, and the game would be replayed at a later date. In essence, that teacher-coach wanted her pitcher to throw the game. My daughter would have nothing to do with that idea, and she never trusted that coach again. What a horrible example that teacher had set.

If you can't trust a person on small matters, you certainly can't have much confidence on the larger issues either. When it comes to matters of trust, there is no middle ground. Trust is not some value that always pertains to the other guy. It is not a far-off, abstract goal never to be achieved. It starts close to home with a promise kept, an agreement sealed with a handshake, the confidence of a friend you can count on, a spouse who is always there through the good times and the bad. And when it comes to trust, perceptions are as important as reality. We should never put ourselves in positions where what we do *appears* to be dishonest, even if it isn't.

Without trust, we are doomed to chaos and confusion because nothing can work. When we tell our boss that we'll deliver that report by a certain date, do we do so on time? If we tell the landlord that the check's in the mail, is it? When we promise our daughter that we'll take her to that concert, do we do so or do we cancel because of a work-related conflict?

Do we warn our children about the dangers of drugs and then go out and drink too much? Do we tell our teenagers to drive carefully and then get a ticket for speeding?

Trust binds people and nations together. It is based on truth. I offer this challenge for anyone who wants to see our nation return to a position of greatness.

Never, ever tell a single lie again!

If we only do that, we will see a new era of prosperity and renewal.

Chapter 8

Humility

Watch Out for Pride

I am no longer your professor,
I am your humble servant.

JUNÍPERO SERRA
Mallorca, 1743

Faith Keeper

We all have transforming moments—times of crisis, of decision, change or great joy. It is during these important thresholds that we know God is present.

It is He who has chosen to be close, to be with us and so such times become important moments of commitment, of consecration. They give us new life, added hope and a world of possibilities.

These are times of special humility where we count our blessings, confess our sins and recommit to His way.

DR. ROBERTA HESTENES
Senior Pastor
Solana Beach (California) Presbyterian Church

From the moment I arrived in Spain as U.S. ambassador, I had wanted to visit Petra, the birthplace of Father Junípero Serra, the humble priest who founded twenty-one missions in California in the late eighteenth century. Having lived almost twenty years in San Diego, where in 1769 Father Serra established his first mission (La Misión de Alcalá), I had special ties with this brave man who had traveled halfway around the globe to serve his Franciscan order as a New World missionary.

As a symbol of the links he created between Spain and the United States, I had brought with me a key to the hand-carved, tall wooden doors of Serra's San Diego mission, whose beauty comes from its absolute simplicity. My plan was to present the key to the curator of the Serra museum on my first visit to Mallorca, a Mediterranean island off the eastern coast of Spain.

One Solitary Man of God

It is difficult to believe that such a humble missionary man born in 1713 in a tiny *pueblecito* (small village) in the center of an island would have such a profound influence. But indeed he did, and today, 250 years later, California is a living testimony to the life of one missionary who dedicated himself to God and to his church. (I realize that the "politically correct" police view him less favorably, but I just happen to disagree with them!)

Father Junípero Serra reminds us all that humility and grace are personal values to be admired, and they can be a powerful force for good.

At age fifteen, Miguel José (Father Serra's given names) was invested as a Franciscan monk, and for fifty-four years he wore with pride the garb of Francis of Assisi. In honor of this humble mentor, Miguel took on the given name of Junípero, who had been Francis's constant companion.

Father Serra grew up next to a convent whose church was used by his family for worship. In those days churches were often financed by wealthy people in exchange for the construction of family *capillas* (chapels), which often surrounded the interior walls of the church. The church in Petra was built in the early 1600s, a century before Serra was born.

It's somewhat breathtaking for a Californian to visit this church where Father Serra prayed each day. Its chapels bear such names as San Diego, San Francisco, Santa Bárbara, and San Bernardino. Before my very eyes, seven thousand miles from California, were the roots of a huge network of names for cities, parks, roads, schools, and hundreds of other places in the west. And all of it had been inspired long ago by one lonely missionary who walked up and down the region we now call California, preaching, praying, and founding small churches along the way.

It all had started when Father Serra selected names for some of the twenty-one missions he founded, from San Diego in the south to San Francisco in the north, all bearing the names of those small chapels where he prayed as a young boy. The missions were strategically located a day's walk apart in areas where people lived and needed to pray. Some survived many years. Others were destroyed by fire or inattention. All have now been restored as invaluable parts of California's heritage and the work of this humble man whose name is legendary up and down the west coast.

We forget the basics that underpin everything we do: faith, family, friends. We allow the trappings of life to drown out the fundamentals. Our cars and condos become our security. The power we think we have comes falsely from our work, from our phony social status, from the superficial and very transitory material things we collect along the way.

Robert Raines, a Michigan minister, said it well:

> *Let not success make me arrogant*
> *but rather grateful.*
> *Let not failure make me fearful*
> *but rather wiser.*
> *Let not pain or malice embitter me*

but enlarge my capacity to endure and overcome.
Keep me vulnerable to others
and so to You.

The Lost Art of Humility

Of all the values at our disposal, humility seems to be the least attractive. You don't see many television ads or billboards extolling the virtues of humility, do you? And take a look at contemporary heroes. Few Father Serras, but plenty of trash-talking, high-fiving, stuff-strutting celebrities who seem transfixed by their own images. Sadly, these "heroes" are emulated by young people looking for ways to be cool and accepted.

Being humble is not commercially viable. It does not sell product. It does not attract media attention. The very essence of humility eschews the spotlight. If you want to get ahead in life, you need an agent or an endorsement contract with a sneaker company. Is it any wonder we see youngsters showing disrespect for authority? They have learned well from their heroes who watch out for number one, no matter what.

I don't want to keep picking on professional sports, because I'm a big fan. But I am often appalled at the behavior—on the field and off—of these highly paid men. And I think the companies who endorse them bear some of the responsibility as well. Commercials that flaunt the athlete's high salary or portray him as bigger and more powerful than his employers do not send a good signal to young people. Nor do some of those football players who go out of their way to humiliate their opponents by mocking them in the end zone after touchdowns are scored.

But the athletes only give us an easy target. In truth, all of us need to take a second look at our "humility quotient." For example, do you:

- believe you deserve a raise just because you put another year in?
- get impatient when you have to wait in line?
- expect a pat on the back when you make a donation to your church or favorite charity?
- buy a nicer car, not because you need one but because your neighbor got one?
- daydream about more?
- take credit when you don't deserve it?

These may seem like insignificant things, but it is in the everyday arena that we either take a stand for a simpler, less cluttered life or join the rest of the crowd in living only for ourselves.

Somehow we have to convince ourselves—and our kids—that it is okay not to be rich and famous. We need to strip away all the phony securities and trappings of life. We lean too much on power, influence, financial gains, and material comforts. In the process, we forget who we are and begin to act like someone else.

Have you ever known people who suddenly came into a windfall? Maybe an inheritance or winning the lottery put them into that stratum where they will never again have to worry about money. Despite protestations that they'll still be the same people they always were, usually the opposite takes place. It's a rare individual who stays humble when his or her life takes a sudden propitious turn. But the rest of us need to remember that just because our newfound prosperity is gradual, it doesn't mean we don't change as well. Are you still satisfied with the lifestyle you had when you were first married? If not, why not?

Ask yourself: if something took away all my possessions—my home, my car, my clothes, my savings—would I still be the same person?

I often wonder if one of the reasons for so much intolerance in our culture is that we have become accustomed to having our own way all the time. Our needs and desires have become paramount, so who cares about what others think? Humility helps us to see the best in others. It helps us to be more tolerant, more forgiving, more modest about our own achievements, however significant we think they might be.

Humility Earns Respect

One of the great ironies of life is that some of the most famous and respected people in the world are also the most humble. Yet we seldom pattern our lives after them. A modest priest from Communist-controlled Poland rises to head his church and becomes the champion of peace around the world. Mother Teresa prays for love and understanding and gives hope to thousands. Yet I don't see a rush toward the priesthood or the convent in America.

Dr. Billy Graham, using simultaneous translations in 150 languages and dialects, beams his messages by satellite, thus reaching billions everywhere. He is probably the best-known figure in the world and is consistently ranked as one of the ten most respected men in the world. And yet Dr. Graham is basically a simple country preacher. He has lived most of his life in a modest home in the mountains of North Carolina. Each day, he prays on his knees as a reminder of his humbleness before the Lord. Nothing illustrates the evangelist's sense of humility more poignantly than the time when a restaurant waitress, obviously flustered to find that she was serving a person she held in awe, dropped her tray, spilling food and dishes everywhere. Dr. Graham immediately jumped up to help her pick up the mess.

I have been blessed to count among my friends dozens of world-class leaders. What stands out in many of their survey responses, featured in the "On the Record" sidebars throughout this book, is their modesty and humility. Most polled gave humble thanks to parents, family, friends,

On the Record

I never looked with favor on executives and others writing books about their lives and achievements while they are still in the midst of their professional careers and productive years. I do not agree with anyone singing his or her praises, much less doing some preaching.

ROBERTO GOIZUETA
Chairman and CEO,
Coca-Cola Company
Atlanta, Georgia

My personal philosophy is quite simple. I am responsible for me and must oversee with great sensitivity the impact of what I say and/or do on others.

BARBARA JORDAN
Former congresswoman and college professor

and key mentors for the important influences they had on their lives. Virtually all cited religious faith as underpinning whatever successes they might have gained along the way. They seldom took credit for their achievements.

Some left positions of enormous power and influence, and they did so gracefully. They had been humble while exercising their authority, and so their transition to a more private life was eased. No one illustrates this point better than Lech Walesa, Poland's longtime freedom fighter who became his country's first democratically elected president. After leading his nation to freedom, and then serving as its leader, Walesa has chosen to return to the same shipyard where he rose from obscurity in 1980 to lead the Solidarity movement that eventually toppled Poland's old Soviet-backed government. Today he works for a salary of about two hundred dollars a month. Despite his successes, including a Nobel Peace Prize and an honorary degree from Harvard University along the way, Walesa never forgot his modest roots. He and Father Serra would have been good friends.

Profiles in Humility

During my years at *The Miami Herald*, three people from very different backgrounds symbolized for me the power of grace and humility. One ministers to 300,000 desperately poor peasants in Peru. Another fled Cuba in a thirteen-foot wooden rowboat and now runs a small gas station in South Miami; and the third is a distinguished federal judge who has been consistently ranked among the top jurists in the Southeast.

First to Lima, for a meeting of Latin American publishers. As I sat in the comfortable hotel room, I thought about the thousands of desperately poor people who live in cardboard huts in the hills surrounding the Peruvian capital. I wanted to see for myself what life was like in this area, commonly known as *pueblos jóvenes* (young towns). This day, my dose of humility would come in a horrible slum town southeast of Peru's major city.

After being turned down by two taxi drivers who considered the trip too dangerous, I arrived at Villa el Salvador, a grim shantytown with a population of more than 300,000. As I stepped out of the cab, I learned about a priest who ministered to the pueblo.

Father Kirk lives on about five hundred dollars a year, some received as contributions from his home parish near Dublin, Ireland, and the rest earned from the sale of chairs he carves in his own hut. Most of the time, though, he ministers to the huge world of people with little hope who live in fifty thousand shacks lined up in rows and separated by dusty roads. That day, Father Kirk invited me to join him on a house call to a bedridden invalid who had broken his back in a thirty-three-foot fall at a construction site. Stretched out on an old door that substituted for a hospital bed, and with his epileptic wife and me at his side, this pathetic person in constant pain received communion from the priest.

As we left, Father Kirk told me that more than anything else, the crippled worker wanted a soldering iron so that he could pass the miserable hours of his life making jewelry. I gave the priest all the money I had—twenty dollars.

Two years later, I received a small pin made with a simple marble and a safety pin. The tattered envelope apparently had been dropped in the mail by a Peruvian passing through Miami's airport. The gift was a wonderful expression of gratitude from a humble man and his equally modest priest.

> ## On the Record
>
> *Long before anyone invented the term "women's lib," Bill liberated me to be a homemaker, wife, and mother. My main accomplishment was raising five little Grahams and watching them grow through good times and bad to be men and women committed to the Lord's service, all as pilgrims in progress.*
>
> *My parents taught me that a sense of humor is the balance wheel of life. Have you ever met a fanatic with a sense of humor?*
>
> RUTH BELL GRAHAM
> Montreat, North Carolina

Gracias a Dios (Thanks to God)

Rubén Pol's story is equally dramatic. Humbled by the crushing onslaught of communism in his native Cuba, Rubén escaped with six other teenagers in a thirteen-foot rowboat. After two days drifting at sea, the penniless group was picked up by an American ship near the Dominican Republic. Five months later Rubén's young wife and five-month-old son arrived in the United States by way of Spain.

In America, they started from scratch and eventually owned their own small service station in South Miami. Rubén worked on cars, his father-in-law pumped gas, and his wife kept the books. The profits fed the family and put two kids through college, and they did it all with the income from a modest auto service station.

To this day Rubén's modesty touches every customer at the station. He never overcharges, never complains, and never does less than his best. "Thanks to God," he says. He is proud of his business and of his family, and his brand of humility and grace reminds me many times that every success starts from humble roots.

Judge Bill Hoeveler has shown me and many others that humility and modesty can be seen in the power of justice as well. Since his appointment to the federal court in 1977, Judge Hoeveler has earned everyone's respect, from lawyers, jurors, clerks, and marshals to litigants.

They picked the best when Judge Hoeveler was selected to oversee the complex, yearlong trial of Manuel Noriega, the former president of Panama who was convicted and sentenced to life by a jury in Judge Hoeveler's court. Before it was over, even General Noriega grew to respect the judge for his fairness in the courtroom.

Lincolnesque in appearance, this tall jurist epitomizes the best of democracy, and he does so with consummate integrity and grace. A deeply religious person, Judge Hoeveler is far more concerned about where society is headed than he is about the material things in life. He lives modestly and prays before each courtroom appearance. His hero is Thomas Merton, a priest who wrote volumes about humility and the simple life.

His Love of Christ

"It is foolish to seek honors, power, and wealth," Judge Hoeveler told me in my values survey. "While I have reached many different stages in life, such as becoming a lawyer, winning some important cases, and then going on the bench, they seem less important than other values. My most important accomplishment is the accepting of a gift—the love of Christ with the opportunity to grow day by day in His service." Bill Hoeveler exudes a special brand of modesty and humility.

In the world of public service, few have shown greater modesty, mixed with commitment and integrity, than Senator Sam Nunn, the retired, highly respected Georgia Democrat. Still young with outstanding prospects for a bright future, Senator Nunn never let the power and influence of his leadership in Congress overtake his humble roots at home. In the Senate he has left a legacy admired on both sides of the aisle.

"I have tried to uphold the values that America has always stood for—that every individual has worth and is entitled to respect and justice and fundamental freedoms," he told me. "I believe all people should have the right to govern themselves and that we all have a responsibility to both God and country to contribute in securing and maintaining these rights and freedoms for everyone."

Dedicated to his children and wife, Colleen, Sam Nunn learned his key values from his parents, school, and church. "Churches were an important part of life in the community," he wrote in my survey, "and everybody seemed to subscribe to the same general code of honesty, integrity, hard work, respect for others, and a caring responsibility."

Despite the demands of his office, Sam Nunn always found time for

On the Record

As to role models, I have had many from time to time but none for a very long time. My feelings are expressed by a song which goes something like this: "You may not be an angel and you may not go to church, but the good that you do will come back to you and it really don't cost very much."

DAVID PACKARD
Founder, Hewlett-Packard

Some men and women make the world better just by being the kind of people they are. That's what I would like to have accomplished—no great deeds performed, nor heroic tasks completed, nor money-power status. Just being who I am.

JOHN GARDNER
Author and professor
Stanford, California

his family. "Our times together as a family were very important to me." Sam Nunn has earned everyone's respect through hard work and an unpretentious approach to leadership. On the Hill, he became every-one's role model.

Teaching Humility

Do your kids moan and groan when you talk about the tough times you went through when you were a kid? Keep telling those stories. A recent study showed that in those families where Mom and Dad repeat stories of hardship in their youth, the families are healthier. I look at my hum-ble beginnings as a real asset. It started in high school when I washed windows, worked on a house-wrecking crew, and drove a garbage truck to help make ends meet and to save up for college. Those were tough jobs with some very difficult people, but I learned important lessons in life through them.

The temptation is to protect your kids from those tough experiences, but I think we do them a real disservice when we give them such an easy life. Even if your kids don't need to work, they should be encouraged to do so. Manual labor is not menial. It teaches appreciation for services that are often taken for granted, and it teaches discipline and humility. I think that's one of the reasons why ServiceMaster, the leading clean-ing and maintenance company in the world, requires its executives to spend time polishing floors and emptying trash. It not only teaches them the finer points of their business, but it keeps them humble.

Regardless of the line of work you're in, it's very important to put yourself in the shoes of those around you. You're likely to find some incredible examples of courage, perseverance, and humility. Some of the happiest, most satisfied people I know are those with few material possessions and limited authority. Yet, their examples have an amazing way of cutting your own self-importance down to size.

I learned that lesson in a rather humorous way when I first took over as publisher of *The Herald*. Early on, I had announced plans to meet all three thousand full- and part-time employees at the newspaper. My pur-pose was simply to tell them I cared deeply about what they did to make our newspaper one of the best in the country. Most, I think, were interested in what their new boss had to say, and they were entitled to know that I considered everyone to be a part of the team. With nine editions and advance sections printed around the clock, it took me almost three months and 153 meetings to get around the main newspaper plant and its three dozen distribution centers located as far as seventy-five miles from our downtown facility. At one of the meetings, which started at 2:00 A.M. so I could reach those on the night shift, I laid out my plans for our newspaper and told those assembled how proud I was to be part of their team and how much I counted on them to get the job done. At the end of my informal comments I always invited questions, and with that, a hand popped up way in the back of the room. "Sir," the man asked, "I arrived a little late and didn't get your name. Just what do you do around here anyway?" He probably had been ordered to attend, but he had a job to do and the last thing he wanted was a speech in the middle of the night. Importantly, this staffer reminded me that I was working for him just as much as he was working for me.

> ## On the Record
>
> *Society undoubtedly needs the media to play a dynamic watchdog role. Nevertheless, watchdogs sometimes bay at the moon and disturb the neighborhood; strew garbage over the front lawn; can be obsessed by the scent of sex; invade the privacy of the neighbor's garden and, alas, they have been known to bite innocent passersby.*
>
> A friend who used this anonymous quote to keep me humble

Humility is an important factor in effective leadership, and that man in the back of the room reminded me of that reality. So did NBC anchorman Tom Brokaw in a speech to journalists: "In American journalism we are inclined to call attention to everyone's failings but our own. In Washington, reporters are often afflicted with Newsheimer's disease, an affliction that causes you to remember everyone's mistakes but your own."

Failure can also provide particularly brutal lessons in humility. Bruce Babbitt, former governor of Arizona and secretary of the interior in the Clinton administration, ran as a candidate for president in 1988. His campaign was candid, informal—and short-lived. What stood out to me, however, was what he said after it was over. "In a way it's been a bonus. You see, my kids have always seen me as a success. Now, I'm not a Super Dad. They see me come home, beaten up, tired, dejected. They've learned I need them. That's real life."

Acknowledging failure is tough, but that's part of being a humble person. President Kennedy had the humility and grace to admit he had made a terrible mistake in approving the abortive Bay of Pigs attack on Cuba, and the country forgave him. On the other hand, Richard Nixon couldn't bring himself to ask forgiveness for the sins of Watergate, and he paid the price.

Sometimes, a good sense of humor goes a long way toward promoting humility. I hope your family enjoys a good laugh together, and I hope you're big enough to be the butt of a joke now and then. Too many parents, especially dads, take themselves so seriously that they come off as being arrogant. Lighten up, and don't be afraid to laugh at your mistakes.

During my years at the Pentagon, a few key aides and I attended early-morning briefings where we reviewed all the night messages that had arrived from military commands around the globe. In this way, we'd be better prepared to help Mel Laird deal with the day's crises. Almost always, someone in that group was in trouble, especially the two responsible for press relations and legislative affairs. "Okay," Mel would ask, "who's in the barrel today?" Invariably, I had the honors, since my job was to keep Congress in tow. As time passed, this meeting became known as the "Barrel Group." We took our work very seriously, but a laugh along the way helped us survive some deadly serious moments. We learned under some very tough, humbling circumstances that to have a sense of humor is not disrespectful of life's problems but rather is a lifesaver in dealing with moments of death and defeat.

When I left the Pentagon in 1971, I gave Mel Laird a small wooden barrel with a metal replica of the Defense Secretary's official flag attached. On the stand that held the unique trophy on his desk was a very formal inscription saying, "The Melvin R. Laird Barrel, awarded daily for extrameritorious screwups." Not to be outdone, Mel returned that barrel to me twenty years later when I was sworn in as U.S. ambassador to Spain. He wanted to be sure I would remain humble.

I've had some pretty heady experiences in life, but whenever I get caught up in myself, I pull out this little poem. I've never found out who wrote it, which seems appropriate, but it really gets to the heart of why we must never think too highly of ourselves.

Sometime, when you're feeling important,
Sometimes, when your ego's in bloom,
Sometimes, when you take it for granted,
You're the best qualified in the room,
Sometimes, when you feel that your going
Would leave an unfillable hole,
Just follow this simple instruction,
And see how it humbles your soul.
Take a bucket and fill it with water,
Put your hand in it, up to the wrist,
Pull it out, and the hole that's remaining,
Is a measure of how you'll be missed.
You may splash all you please when you enter,
You can stir up the water galore,
But stop and you'll find in a minute,
That it looks quite the same as before.
The moral in this quaint example
Is do the best that you can,
Be proud of yourself but remember,
There is no indispensable man.

Chapter 9

Perseverance

"Quit" Is a Four-Letter Word

We shall go to the end, we shall fight in France, we shall fight on the seas and oceans, we shall fight with growing confidence and growing strength in the air, we shall defend our island, whatever the cost may be, we shall fight on the beaches, we shall fight on the landing grounds, we shall fight in the fields and in the streets, we shall fight in the hills, we shall never surrender.

WINSTON CHURCHILL
Radio address, 1940

Faith Keeper

The problem with most leaders today is they don't stand for anything. Leadership implies movement toward something, and convictions provide the direction. If you don't stand for something, you'll fall for anything.

DON SHULA
NFL head coach

Years after World War II, Winston Churchill was asked to address Harrow, a prestigious prep school he attended as a boy. The students were warned to bring pencil and paper and to take copious notes; the grand old man was soon to arrive. Much to everybody's surprise, the address was only six words: "Never give up. Never. Never. Never." Like his famous radio address in Britain's darkest hour, the former prime minister's message was very simple. Commitment is everything.

The hero of World War II got right to the point, didn't he?

No one did a better job of hanging in there than Winston Churchill. At age thirty-seven, after a string of early successes in his career, he was discredited as first lord of the admiralty. Later, he lost two successive elections, then returned to office in 1924. Five years later, he was again run out of office, this time in the wake of an economic downturn. It wasn't until age sixty-six that Churchill's greatest moment came—as leader of his country on the brink of defeat at the hands of the Germans.

Perseverance was Churchill's middle name. He never gave up, never admitted defeat, even as the enemy overran his troops. And his was much more than a personal act of perseverance—he had driven his own personal commitment into the soul of every last Englishman. Through sheer determination and persistence, Churchill had converted a nation of despair into one of hope.

I'd like to tell you that it will be easy getting our country back on the right course. But the truth is, nothing that matters is easy. The important things we want to do in life require hard work, perseverance, and a good dose of Providence. If you're not in it for the long haul, you're really not in it.

For NFL coaching great Vince Lombardi, success was impossible without persistence:

After the cheers have died and the stadium is empty, after

the headlines have been written and after you are back in
the quiet of your own room and the Super Bowl ring has
been placed on the dresser and all the pomp and fanfare
have faded, the enduring things that are left are: The dedi-
cation to excellence; the dedication to victory; and the dedi-
cation to doing with our lives the very best we can to make
the world a better place in which to live.

Despite very different lines of work, Churchill and Lombardi were in the same league. They were driven to excel, and they did so by hanging in there, despite the odds. As Jim Michener once put it, "Character consists of what you do on the third and fourth tries."

Running When You Have No Feet

Talk about trying, I'd like to introduce you to Tony Volpentest, a young athlete I met during the 1992 Barcelona Paraolympics Games. Through sheer courage and willpower, Tony walked off with two new world records that earned him gold medals in the 100-meter and 200-meter track events and a silver medal in the 4 X 100-meter relay.

Tony was born without hands or feet.

Growing up in Washington state, Tony Volpentest wanted more than anything to be just like his buddies. He refused to feel sorry for himself, charging ahead with the strong encouragement of family and friends. As one of his coaches said, "Someone forgot to tell Tony he doesn't have all his parts."

Tony could have given up as a youngster and no one would have blamed him. He started his running career using regular prostheses but graduated to high-tech devices because one of his legs ends just below the knee, the other just below the ankle. He now uses special graphite legs, and to prop his arms on the starting line for his races, he uses two paint cans topped with foam padding. From there, it's been on to one victory after another.

"You can do anything you want in life if you want it badly enough," Tony told me. Think about Tony the next time you feel like giving up.

Against the Odds

Don't you just love to hear about people who charge forward against incredible odds? The walk-on, skinny college freshman determined to make the college football team. The kid with cancer who talks himself well despite the pain and grim outlook. The parents who struggle through the highs and lows of raising their kids. The very average student who gets good grades through just plain hard work. The ordinary worker, with very average job skills, who plugs along putting in a good day's work, every day. No matter how tough it gets, such people always manage to persevere. And their stories inspire us.

Babe Ruth struck out 1,330 times on his way to 714 home runs. R. H. Macy failed seven times before his store caught on in New York. Thomas Edison tested fifty thousand compounds before he perfected a new storage battery. As he said many times, "Genius is 1 percent inspiration and 99 percent perspiration." With it, he had created the phonograph, electric light bulb, and motion-picture camera. Perseverance paid off.

Legendary Spanish author Miguel de Cervantes spent most of his adult life fighting debt and misfortune. In war, he was captured by pirates, held captive for five years, and wounded so seriously that he could never again use his left arm. From there he was taken to be a slave of a Greek renegade in Algiers, where he unsuccessfully tried to escape three times and was finally ransomed in 1575.

Later, Cervantes held two government jobs and failed at both. At fifty-three he was back in prison, where he decided to write a book. Finally, after a half-century of perseverance, he hit the jackpot—with *Don Quixote*, a book that has captured the world's imagination for over 350 years.

When figure skater Kristi Yamaguchi fell down during the 1992 Winter Olympics, some felt her chances of winning the gold had evaporated in an instant. But not Kristi, who spent several days with us during the Summer Olympics in Barcelona later that year. She simply picked herself up off the ice and skated on as if nothing had happened. Her performance, otherwise flawless, earned her the gold medal. Not even a bad fall could destroy Kristi's determination to hang in there.

So You're Not a Figure Skater

Okay, so you don't have to lace up the skates and take to the spotlight of an Olympic skating rink. You still have to do something just as important. Your Olympics may be a tough job. Impossible assignments. Cranky customers. Or your marriage may be one of those that just take a lot of hard work. And as a parent, I know that raising kids can seem a lot harder than winning Super Bowls.

So the first thing I want you to do is give yourself a big pat on the back. You've made it this far, and that's worth celebrating. Just because you haven't climbed Mount Everest or gotten inducted into some Hall of Fame doesn't mean you don't have (or need) perseverance. In fact, it's usually the ordinary trials of life that demand the most perseverance. Hang in there!

Naturally, all of us need to work on this because, let's face it, one of the reasons our nation is experiencing so many problems is that we've let our guard down. Good parents who know better let some of their standards slide when it comes to guiding their children. They start out trying to hold the line on movies and television viewing but get worn down with "Debbie's mom lets her see R-rated movies." So while I think you need a pat on the back for doing so well thus far, I urge you to recommit yourself to the various responsibilities you face.

There's no secret to building persistence in your life. As the Nike commercial used to say, just do it. But here are some things that tend to keep you pushing on when the going gets tough.

Respect for the Obstacles. Fear of failure is natural and can be managed to your advantage. Instead of letting your anxieties get you down, let them work *for* you. Let's face it. A little healthy fear keeps you going. Denying it only makes it worse. Think of yourself as a mountain climber. Healthy fear encourages you to keep going but to be careful and make sure you do the job right. That shouldn't be your sole motivation, but it doesn't hurt to be a little bit afraid of what's ahead of you.

Encouragement. Unfortunately, you don't have much control over this in your own life, but when encouragement comes your way, don't brush it off or ignore it. Take courage from a colleague's words of encouragement. On the other hand, become an encourager to others. Maybe you can give some to your kids or colleagues to help them persevere. I hung in there many times because others encouraged me—high-school teachers, a hard-working mother who brought me up on a modest secretary's salary, and a few special friends who became very important mentors during those impressionable teenage years.

When I am invited to speak at a convention or other event, I sometimes place blank cards on the tables. At the end of my talk I ask the audience to think about someone who has helped them in the past, and I encourage them to use the cards for notes to such friends. You'd be amazed how special it is to receive such a note, especially when it isn't expected. Can you think of some people in your life who encouraged you at a particularly difficult time? Write them a note or, better yet, call them.

> ## On the Record
>
> *As a young Cuban refugee, I went from riches to rags in a forty-five-minute airplane trip. I would like to be remembered as a humanitarian who always found the good side of people.*
>
> TERE ZUBIZARETTA
> Cuban refugee and
> advertising agency owner
>
> *Impossible is not a word in my vocabulary. By leadership, example, and encouragement, I have enabled others to achieve far beyond their expectations.*
>
> BILL LEE
> Former chairman and CEO,
> Duke Power
> Charlotte, North Carolina

CNN president Tom Johnson, a longtime friend who has earned everyone's admiration in the media business, knows better than most what that pat on the back means to young people. Tom attended college and graduate school on full scholarships provided by the owner of the local newspaper in his hometown, Macon, Georgia. With this all-important boost, Tom went on to become a White House fellow and, later, publisher of the *Los Angeles Times*. His generous mentor in Georgia had given him his first break in life. "Through this experience," Tom told me, "I learned the importance of being a champion to young people who strive to make it in life."

The Big Picture. Big problems look smaller when you stand back and get an overview. Sometimes you just need to see your problem from a higher perspective. Author and pastor Kent Hughes once told his congregation to imagine themselves first at the top of the church steeple looking down, then on a cloud, then on the moon, then in another galaxy. You get the picture. Seen from a wider view, your problems look smaller and it's easier to stick with it.

Inspiration. One thing that kept many of the Vietnam War POW's from giving up was thinking about their families back home. Focusing on something important to you gives you inspiration. When you're about to give up, think of your children or your spouse. If you're tempted to give in to an unrealistic demand from one of your children, try to picture that child graduating from college. Let that image inspire you to do what's right.

Enthusiasm. Another important companion to perseverance is enthusiasm. Enthusiasm lifts the spirits. It fuels a zest for life. In fact, enthusiasm can extend life. You might think people are born with enthusiasm, but that's not true. It's an attitude, a choice. It's a deliberate approach to life that you can adopt to help you persevere. As you face a difficult task, give yourself permission to get excited about it. Find something good in that project to look forward to, even if it's only getting the thing over with!

Belief in God. For me, the best inspiration comes from above. I firmly believe in the power of prayer and meditation to help you persevere. Faith in God gives you strength beyond your own ability. And quiet times reflecting on your beliefs will help you stand firm when you might otherwise feel like giving up. I'm not a proponent of school prayer, and I support the constitutional separation of church and state. But I don't think that means we should never be public about our beliefs. I can assure you that as a newspaper publisher I relied on prayer to guide my work.

Persistence Pays Off

You might get the idea that I'm promoting some nebulous concept that does little more than make people feel good. Aside from the fact that I'm all for making people feel good, there's a bigger payoff: it works. Sticking with the right course of action no matter what the obstacles results in a better life. For example, I believe it's no accident that crime rates went down in 1995. It's the result of hundreds of local programs all across America. At every level of government and society, we made reduction of crime a priority. Even with money scarce and a constantly moving target, we stayed the course and are now seeing progress. Police departments are being beefed up. Potential criminals are given help before they get in trouble. Drug abusers are being rehabilitated. Kids are being taught to solve their problems without resorting to violence.

The long and often troubled road to peace in the Middle East is another example of how persistence pays off. So many times since that historic signing of a peace accord on the White House lawn in September 1993, the Israelis and Palestinians could have easily walked away from the process. No one would have blamed the Israelis for quitting after Prime Minister Rabin was assassinated. But they held on to even the smallest strands of hope and are making progress toward settling the tough issues that have led to so much violence.

On the Record

I believe in doing exactly what you say you're going to do: in dedication to carefully analyzed goals, in calm resolution of adversity, in the Golden Rule. In short, honesty, reliability, and accountability.

SUE COBB
Attorney and member,
1988 Mount Everest Expedition
Miami, Florida

My accomplishments? Founding Sun Microsystems, my boy, Maverick, and shooting a seventy in golf.

SCOTT MCNEALY
CEO, Sun Microsystems
Mountain View, California

Think of what would happen in our own country if we had that kind of stick-with-it attitude. Think of how our society might improve if we made a commitment to not let anything prevent us from solving some of our toughest problems. Yes, family life is falling apart and divorce rates have soared. Tonight, more than 40 percent of our children will go to sleep without a father in the house. Some inner cities have illegitimate birthrates in excess of 80 percent, and their neighborhoods are in chaos because no men are around as positive role models. If the children in this environment are to have any chance in life, everyone must do something to help. In many instances we must create a substitute sense of family through our schools, churches, and social organizations. Every intact family needs to hang in there, and every social institution needs to persevere in helping broken families.

Yes, it's true that many jobs have been eliminated by corporate America, but in the long run that will make American business more competitive, which in turn will create additional jobs as we sell our goods and services in the global marketplace. It's already happening, and those men and women who retooled and upgraded their skills are being rewarded for their persistence. Never give up if you lose your job!

I agree that we have a crisis in public education in this country. Test scores are down; many children are no longer safe. And many parents feel they are losing control of what goes on in the classroom. Does pulling out of the system do any good? Don't give up so easily. Get involved. Go to school-board meetings. Develop relationships with teachers and administrators. Be part of a solution. Persevere. That's the only way it will get better.

It's very unlikely that we will solve all our current social problems in my lifetime, and even if we did, we would have a brand-new set of problems on which to work. So it makes no sense to retreat, build bigger houses, and try our best to insulate ourselves from the real world. Never give up.

The Paralysis of Inaction

Sometimes we give up before we ever start. The prospect of the challenge at hand is so daunting that we just decide we can't do it. I can understand that; in fact, I would be tempted to do that if I had Dr. Barth Green's job.

Dr. Green is the founder of the Miami Project to Cure Paralysis. Most would think that's a no-win job. I mean, if the spinal cord is severed, that's about all she wrote, right? Well, not for the doctor. Surrounded by hundreds of patients with near-fatal spinal cord injuries,

Barth Green has been determined to find answers through research, surgery, brain-cell transplants, and computerized rehabilitation known as patterning. Nearly all his patients, who come from all over the world seeking help, could be categorized as hopeless cases. But with all the technology and research, Dr. Green relies on one simple word: perseverance. That little finger may not move when you try to lift it, but keep trying. He knows that you cannot overcome any disability if you have given up. Attitude counts.

Years ago when I was serving on a destroyer in the Pacific, the officer who filled out my annual fitness report told me I'd never make it as a leader. From the beginning, our chemistry was bad and I guess it showed. But at sea, his conventional wisdom was law and I was just a lowly ensign. His criticism was very tough, and I thought somewhat unfair, but even then there are lessons to be learned. If nothing else, his words gave me strong reasons to persevere. I was going to prove to myself that this guy's "conventional wisdom" was wrong. No matter what, I was going to hang in there.

Such persistence is also necessary when standing up for what you believe, especially when it flies against the majority. That was very much the situation in 1984 when I found myself battling my own editorial board on the issue of whom our newspaper would endorse that year for president. I felt strongly that *The Herald* should back the Reagan-Bush ticket, but most of the board preferred Mondale-Ferraro.

For me, it was one of those moments that defines leadership authenticity. My credibility would have been zero if the newspaper I was responsible for had selected a candidate I could not support.

The public is entitled to know where a newspaper stands on such matters even though, in the case of presidential endorsements, most have made up their minds long before their newspaper takes a stand.

> ## On the Record
>
> *I would like to be remembered for being a loving and supporting husband and dad; for being available to help people in need, and for allowing the love of Jesus to play a part in a very competitive and tough professional and business career.*
>
> FRANK DRACHMAN, JR.
> Engineering contractor
> San Diego, California

Many publishers abdicate this duty to their editors, and I felt in this case that such an approach would be wrong, especially since I was a regular participant in editorial board meetings.

When the informal vote was in, more than three-quarters of the board wanted Mondale. They were up in arms with my decision. Some wanted to quit and urged me to pass up endorsing at all. I thought that would have been a cop-out.

What I did, though, was to encourage our editorial page editor, Jim Hampton, to use his Sunday column to present his case, and I would state mine in my column. Alongside would be the formal editorial endorsement. I thought this move, somewhat unprecedented in the business, was a triple play of authenticity.

Many of our readers were dismayed. We received hundreds of letters and calls in the days that followed. Those who agreed with the endorsement of Reagan-Bush thought I was a wimp because I didn't fire the entire majority. Those who disagreed felt I was unbelievably arrogant . . . and that I should be fired. On balance, though, the readers loved the fight mostly because they had gained some insight into the dynamics of the editorial endorsement process.

It was tough to buck my colleagues. We had worked closely and cared deeply about the role of our editorial pages, especially on important local matters, where we had significant impact. I'd like to tell you that I knew ahead of time how all my decisions would play out, but I can't. What I learned is that we must stand up for what we believe. Even if you are proven wrong, you can look yourself in the mirror. After all, no one respects a person who vacillates or who doesn't have the guts to take a stand.

One of the most moving messages of perseverance in recent years has come from the popular movie *Forrest Gump*, the wonderful story of a very average young boy with an equally modest intelligence. When Forrest's mother was told by her son's counselor that he had a low IQ, she refused to accept that as a limitation. She wasn't about to let some crummy grammar-school adviser write off her son's future, and so she taught her son how to persevere against all odds.

With his mother's constant encouragement, Forrest never gave up. "You can do it," she said time and again. And he did—mostly through persistence and a pat on the back.

You can too, and maybe this poem by Calvin Coolidge will be your pat on the back:

> *Nothing in the world can take the place of persistence.*
> *Talent will not. Nothing is more common than unsuccessful*
>   *men with talent.*
> *Genius will not. Unrewarded genius is almost a proverb.*
> *Education will not. The world is full of educated derelicts.*
> *Persistence and determination alone are omnipotent.*
> *The slogan "Press On" has solved and always will solve the*
>   *problems of the human race.*

Chapter 10

Optimism

Attitude Counts More Than Talent

Attitude, to me, is more important than facts. It is more important than the past, than education, than money, than circumstances, than failures, than successes, than what other people think or say or do. . . .

The remarkable thing is that we have a choice every day regarding the attitude we will embrace for that day. . . . I am convinced that life is 10 percent what happens to me, and 90 percent how I react to it. And so it is with you. We are in charge of our attitudes.

CHARLES SWINDOLL

Faith Keeper

Look for the best in each other, and always do your best to bring it out. Be cheerful no matter what; pray all the time; thank God no matter what happens. This is the way God wants you who belong to Christ Jesus to live.

1 THESSALONIANS 5:15–18
(The Message)

Much to the chagrin of my family, I am one of those obnoxious characters who wake up immediately, full of energy and cheerful comments, proclaiming that it's a beautiful day even in a downpour. My wife and children found such "morning" people rather annoying, but in the end, I think they too came to appreciate that enthusiasm and optimism can be lifesavers.

I realize not everyone is as optimistic, and I've tried to figure out how I was lucky enough to have such a positive outlook. The only thing I can come up with is that it works. I've faced some pretty tough circumstances in my life, and I'm certain I would never have survived if I had gone into each one believing I would fail. Christian author and leader Charles Swindoll is right. Attitude is everything in life.

Finding the "Good Signs"

Many of the optimists I have known had no right to be so positive. All the cards were stacked against them. Sharpened by the struggle, but always believing that they would prevail, they have become the movers and motivators around us.

No one brought home that message with greater meaning than my personal hero, Navy captain Harry Jenkins. Harry spent seven frightening years as a prisoner of war in North Vietnam. He was lucky to have survived his shoot-down over Hanoi in 1965 but, little did he know, life was about to get worse.

Slapped into solitary confinement for fifty months, he was denied food, medical care, mail, and any sense of even basic human dignity. He was tortured repeatedly for refusing to cooperate with the enemy, yet he never lost hope. Harry always found something to laugh about. As horrible as it was, he found joy in simply being alive.

No matter how miserable the conditions of captivity, no matter how brutal the physical and mental torture, Harry Jenkins almost always managed to find something to be cheerful about. He called them Good

Signs. Through faith and optimism, he believed that there is some good in almost everyone, even his captors. If torture resumed, it would be a good sign because it inevitably would end. If the bombing of North Vietnam was stepped up, it was a good sign because that meant the United States was increasing pressure on his captors to settle the war. Christmas was a good sign because it meant one more year closer to release, whenever that might be.

Good Signs from God

Most of the time there were no good signs, so he'd dream them up. In the final months of their captivity, the men were allowed to congregate after dinner. To help pass the time, Harry created Movie Night, a time when he and others would "tell" old movies from memory. Imagine trying to recall a movie you saw seven years ago and then relate it scene by scene. With little effort, he could extend what originally had been a two-hour movie into a five-hour extravaganza, adding amusing characters and chapters to the plot. Some of his buddies told me later that he should have received an Academy Award for his performance.

On the day Harry was let out of his cramped cell after fifty months of solitary confinement, you might expect the reunion with fellow POW's to be rather emotional, to say the least. Not for Harry. After a quick glance into the grim concrete cell next to his, Captain Jenkins mused to the guy who had lived there for over four years, "Nice little place you have here." Forget something profound. Once again, Harry's cheerful attitude had saved the day. Some of his fellow prisoners told me later that Harry's optimism had actually saved their lives.

When Harry Jenkins returned home in 1973, he immediately found more Good Signs, this time with his family, at work, and around his neighborhood. He was incapable of bitterness or cynicism. Despite the fact that the Vietnam captivity had erased seven years of his life, he came home feeling enormously blessed.

What are the Good Signs of your own life? They are always there, but whether or not you find them depends almost entirely on your outlook. If you wake up believing that it will be a lousy day, it certainly will be just that. If you take on a challenge convinced you will fail, you will. Stop right now and list as many Good Signs in your life as you can. Are you healthy? Do you have a job? Did you have enough to eat yesterday? Have you seen a sunset recently? Does your spouse love you? Write one of these good signs on a Post-it™ and stick it on your dashboard on the way to work.

Sometimes we miss the Good Signs because of the "if only" complex: If only I made more money I'd be happy. If only I could lose some weight. If only my teenagers weren't such a handful. If only my spouse understood me better. Yet each of those negative judgments has a positive corollary: At least you've got *some* income, more than enough to eat, active, normal kids, and a spouse. Lots of people have none of these. Turn them into Good Signs and see what happens. Harry Jenkins easily could have let his conditions creep into his attitude, but he didn't. He turned bad things into Good Signs, and you can too.

> **On the Record**
>
> *Let us rekindle the fires of patriotism in the hearts and homes of all our people. Let us light anew the lamp of national pride. For love of country is our greatest wealth, and national pride our greatest strength.*
>
> *If we do these things, our tomorrow can be rich in promise and our children and our children's children can live in peace and freedom . . . under God.*
>
> CHARLES GOULD
> Former publisher,
> San Francisco Examiner

Soaring in Heaven

Sadly, Harry Jenkins was killed in a freak aircraft accident several months after I had written this chapter on optimism. Harry, who spent eight years building the plane in his garage, had flown hundreds of hours in his Long Easy experimental aircraft. Constructing, maintaining, and flying it had been his consuming hobby for two decades. In my office I have a special enlargement of a color photo I took from the rear seat of Harry's plane as we flew west one afternoon toward the setting sun off the coast of California. I have reflected many times on the symbolism represented. Little did I know that it would be my last flight with him. This picture has been my companion throughout the many hours

I spent writing this book. Now, I picture Harry somewhere above — soaring across the skies, tipping his wings for angels while he helps Saint Peter find some Good Signs in heaven. I know for certain he's there.

Develop a Passion for Life

I'm sure you have known people, as have I, who are optimistic even on their deathbeds. They project joy in a life lived well; they focus on others even as their own lives fade. Their passion for living an enthusiastic, optimistic life carries them to the bitter end. Even in death, their example inspires others to appreciate more the joy of each day. Wouldn't that be a great legacy to leave?

Zig Ziglar, author of *See You at the Top*, urges that we kindle the fires of our own optimism this way: "I am a focused, disciplined, enthusiastic, positive-thinking, a decisive extra-miler, who is a competent, energized, self-starting team player determined to develop and use all of these leadership qualities in my personal, family and business life. These are the qualities of the winner I was born to be." It's just about impossible not to be a winner with that outlook!

Father John Powell, a Loyola University professor and author, speaks powerfully about the blessings of life in a book he wrote a generation ago, *Fully Human, Fully Alive*. In it, this humble priest describes fully alive people as those who use positive attitudes "to employ their talents, to live vibrant lives and to do so more concerned about what can go right in their lives rather than what can go wrong."

"Fully alive people," according to Father Powell, "do not see their lives as a perennial funeral procession with one day following uneventfully on the heels of another. Alive people see tomorrow as a new opportunity which they eagerly await. They are on the growing edge of life." I don't know about you, but I want to be on the growing edge.

The Caring Institute puts the power of a full life, lived optimistically, this way:

Keep your thoughts positive because your thoughts become your words.

Keep your words positive because your words become your actions.

Keep your actions positive because your actions become your
  habits.
Keep your habits positive because your habits become your values.
Keep your values positive because your values become your destiny.

The Healing Power of Optimism

Even when people are sick, a positive attitude helps. Medical research
has shown that a sunny outlook can actually improve your health and
help overcome the trauma of terminal disease. In the mid-1960s, author
Norman Cousins became very ill and was given one chance in five hundred of recovery. But he never gave up. Through a positive attitude, he
believed himself well. Cousins used everything from old Marx Brothers
films to positive thinking to cure his incurable blood disease. His example underscores the power of positive attitudes among other survivors of
serious illnesses:
- They all had a strong will to live.
- They were not panicky about their illness.
- They had confidence in their ability to persevere.
- Despite the odds described, they believed they could make it.
- They were convinced that their treatment would work.

Studies have shown that laughter and hopefulness go together.
People who are capable of experiencing joy are much better candidates
for successful surgery and therapy than those who are depressed and
doubtful, according to a recent article in the *New England Journal of
Medicine*. Optimists handle stress better. Optimists recover from surgery
faster. Medical studies have shown that when patients believe that the
outcome will eventually be good, they are more likely to obtain a good
outcome than if they believe it will eventually be bad.

As Cousins said, "We must never underestimate the capacity of the
human mind and body to regenerate, even when the prospects seem
most wretched. Choose positive emotions. They help to combat illness
and serve as an effective blocker to disease. Love, hope, faith, a will to
live, creativity, festivity, laughter, determination, purpose, confidence
are divine powers."

Read that last sentence again. If a positive attitude is an antidote to disease, think of what it can do to something as ordinary as a damaged relationship, a difficult challenge at work, a personal problem. I am not saying that you may never need professional help—Cousins kept his doctors—but don't underestimate the power of optimism.

Enjoy God's Blessings Now

I have friends in their eighties who are vibrant, interested in others, fun to be with, and involved in new challenges every day. Their lives are full of joy and new adventures. They enjoy life and feel stimulated by new interests and new friends. Instead of being selfish and cynical, they are sharing and caring. They refuse to sit around feeling sorry for themselves. Instead, they reach out to help others and, in the process, help themselves.

Good attitudes also can help you through times of change. Newspaper columnist and author Ellen Goodman puts it well. "There's a trick to the Graceful Exit. It begins with the vision to recognize when a job, a life stage, a relationship, is over—and to let go. It means leaving what's over without denying its validity or its past importance in our lives. It involves a sense of future, a belief that every exit line is an entry, that we are moving on rather than out."

I have used this advice dozens of times with good friends who have lost their jobs—midcareer—as a result of bankruptcies or mergers and other strategic consolidations. But you can apply it to any transition in your life. Instead of looking at the downsides of an empty nest, for example, consider all the things you've wanted to do when you had some freedom from your kids. It's all in how you look at your current situation.

Believe me, I think the need for an optimistic spirit is going to grow, thanks to two socioeconomic forces at work today: downsizing and longer, healthier lives. As a result, there is a huge group of people too young to retire and yet in need of new skills to move forward. Think of it this way: if you are over forty, you may find yourself involuntarily retired within fifteen years, yet you'll have at least another twenty years to live well (and pay bills). Who's going to survive: the guy who mopes around grumbling about layoffs, big business, and "old age," or the guy who says, "Hey, this is great. I've always wanted to try something new!"?

Newspapers, believe it or not, also have a key role in generating optimism. When the spirit of the day is negative, communities crumble, leaders fail, and social needs go unmet. I remember an important speech given at an editors' conference by Michael O'Neill, then editor of the *New York Daily News*. Highly respected by his colleagues, Mike gave me important advice just as I began my tour as publisher:

> We should begin with an editorial philosophy that is more positive, more tolerant of the frailties of human institutions and their leaders, more sensitive to the rights and feelings of individuals . . . If we are always downbeat—if we exaggerate and dramatize the negatives in our society—we attack the optimism that has always been a wellspring of American progress.

On the Record

My family seems to exhibit certain common characteristics: sensitivity, a sense of fairness, compassion, sophistication, humor, and a love of animals.

GEORGE GALLUP, JR.
The Gallup Polls
Princeton, New Jersey

I want to be remembered for providing a sense of perspective—an awareness that many of the things that society tends to get wrought up about are in fact trivial or silly.

DAVE BARRY
Columnist and author,
The Miami Herald

Lifting Our Nation's Spirits

No one did a better job of instilling a sense of optimism than President Ronald Reagan. For eight years he worked successfully to help America feel good about itself. He proved that optimism was a powerful force for the good of the individual, and for the good of our country. Though frequently criticized as being too much of a pollyanna with that positive approach, President Reagan did in fact change our country's attitudes. He lifted our national spirit and conveyed a sense of optimism that helped us improve. That optimism led to commitment, and that, from a national security standpoint, pushed the old USSR over the brink. For almost a generation, certainly since the end of World War II, a powerful group of liberals had lost their commitment to a strong America. They wanted us to plead for settlements with our adversaries, even as those adversaries were arming themselves to the teeth. When the Russians stood firm, believing that we were weak of will, key members of Congress proposed that we proceed to disarm unilaterally on the theory that our good deeds would inspire similar action by our adversaries. This crowd was wrong. Dead wrong, as the events of the Reagan and Bush years have shown.

No checklist will turn you into an optimist. But I've used the following to inspire myself, and perhaps it will inspire you.

Ultimate Fulfillment Through God

- Optimists see faith in God as their only way to ultimate fulfillment.

- Optimists have great love for others, starting with family and close friends.

- Optimists always look for the good in others.

- Optimists are cheerful, always seeking a favorable twist to the world around them.

- Optimists laugh a lot. They laugh at themselves too.

- Optimists see Good Signs everywhere. They believe in the power of a smile.

- Optimists love what they do, and they put all their heart into it.

- Optimists count their blessings, one at a time—sometimes daily as a means of overcoming pessimism.

- Optimists learn to forgive, thus minimizing the paralyzing emotions of anger, hate, and selfishness.

- Optimists have can-do attitudes. They refuse to let unfavorable odds get them down.

- Optimists believe in change and welcome new challenges.

- Optimists take charge of their futures.

- Optimists look forward to what the future holds, working along the way to understand better how young people think.

- Optimists do everything possible to avoid negative thoughts.

- Optimists do not dwell on problems they can do nothing about. They are more accepting of things they cannot change.

- Optimists take chances. They dream. They refuse to surrender.

- Optimists do everything possible to avoid cynics. They speak a different language.

- Optimists use the power of positive and confident attitudes to think themselves well.

- Optimists are not born. They are molded by their own attitudes.

We all know people who have such joyful approaches to life. We need to let their example serve to inspire us as we shape our own.

Optimism counts!

Chapter 11

Self-Renewal

Freshen Up Your Life

A man can hold high office, command great powers, and be hailed as the leader of the world, but when his time in office is over he must be prepared mentally, emotionally, spiritually, to relinquish the power, the prestige and the public acclaim that came with the office.

He must retain the quiet confidence that he has been the same man all along and that whatever he contributed as President he can still contribute in other ways.

This is not an easy transition to make, but with the help of one's family and one's friends, and with the conviction that God works His own purposes in each of our lives, it is easier to see that leaving the White House is not the end of the world, but simply the beginning of a new chapter in one's life.

PRESIDENT GERALD FORD
Commencement Address, 1977

Faith Keeper

A chapter is being written in your life today. How will it read?

The Daily Walk

Years ago, Ernie Arbuckle, a good friend and much-beloved business leader in California, told me that a meaningful life requires that we repot from time to time. Like clockwork, he had done so every ten years. Early in his career he became dean of Stanford University's Graduate School of Business with the understanding, up front, that he would not stay a day longer than ten years. He lived up to his word after making that institution one of the nation's best. Then he moved on to become a leading bank president and, later, chairman of a billion-dollar food-service company. Each tour was fixed in length and he succeeded in each. The changes were invigorating. As President Ford once said, "Change is not the end of the world. It's simply the beginning of the next chapter."

Ernie was one of those special people whom we respect and seek out for advice when it's time to make important decisions in life. When it came to career moves, he'd get right to the bottom line of the key issues involved. Usually his answer was, Go for it. Renew your life. Author Jim Michener put the concept this way: "If you are lucky in life, you'll meet someone who will enlarge your horizon. Then you'll realize there's another whole world out there. If you don't, you may miss the whole ball game."

Ernie didn't want his friends to miss the ball game.

Don't Wait for Change

Too many of us do not have the courage to take the plunge into new adventures, and yet that is often exactly what we need to do. We get in ruts, we perform poorly at work, our marriages become shaky, and we drift from one boring day to the next. In the process, we act as if we will live forever, wasting one precious day after the next. Procrastination is the easy way out, and so we live as if tomorrow is a certainty.

Counting on what might happen in the future is a dangerous game.

I have this little theory. Most reading this have, at one time or another, thought of making a deliberate change in your career. Maybe right this moment you're thinking, "Gee, if I could do it I would quit my job and try . . ." Do you know why you decided to stay where you are? Because you're uncertain about the future. Will I make it? Will there be enough money? Will I give up security? I can assure you, if you change directions in your life the answer to all three questions is a resounding "Yes!" (And don't let security ever dictate your options—these days, no one has security.)

Whenever I have made a major move in my life, I have always found even more interesting options out there than I initially thought possible. No matter how many adventures I've been blessed with, there's still a huge world waiting to be discovered. By sharpening your focus, you most likely will put added meaning into your life and the personal values that drive it.

Turn to Prayer

Self-renewal involves a willingness to make changes in your life, often resulting in major adjustments in career, lifestyle and the like. Such changes can be traumatic but the end result can be uplifting. In my life, I have never gone through such thresholds without turning to the Lord in prayer. Where should I settle after my tour in the Navy? Is this the right person to become my marriage partner for life? Will our newborn children be healthy? Is it right for me to drag my family across country for yet another career move? "Lord, give me the courage to face these decisions, and guide my decisions," I would pray.

It's tough to do. We all worry too much and we are unwilling to turn our decisions and problems over to God for guidance and reassurance. But we must.

The challenge of change was very much on my mind in February 1993 as I wrapped up my ambassadorial duties in Madrid. Soon my time as an American ambassador would be nothing more than a cherished memory, and all the perquisites of diplomacy and foreign service would disappear. Gone would be the sizable staff who helped with our ambassadorial duties. No more Marine guards. No more limousines, no police security, no entourage to shadow my every move. In an instant, I'd shift from being

Mr. Ambassador to Mr. Ordinary, carrying my bags and answering my own phone as I returned to the real world. Talk about repotting!

By tradition and protocol, my ambassadorial duties would officially end the moment our jet was airborne. And so, quite symbolically, my final salute to the country we had grown to love would be Wheels Up. *Hasta muy pronto, España.* (Loosely translated: We'll be back soon, Spain.)

As I watched the west coast of Spain disappear behind us over the Atlantic, I thought about the exciting opportunities ahead: the new adventures and priorities, the new goals, the renewal of my commitments to my wife and our family. It was time to move on and start over again. As I have learned so many times before, change is exhilarating. I'm still learning things about life that I might have never learned had I stayed with the first job I ever had.

On the Record

I am blessed with a close and wonderful family, and I want to spend the rest of my life letting them know how much I love them and appreciate them. One of my most important accomplishments, one I am still working on, is to be a huge success in the grandfather business. I would like to be remembered for integrity, service, and family.

GEORGE BUSH
Houston, Texas
1995

Thrive, Don't Survive

Don't be afraid of change, whether you initiate it or whether it's imposed on you. Sure, there will be some discomfort, but repotting also puts you in some new, fresh soil. You'll meet new friends. You'll vary your routines. Even mundane things like getting a new office, learning a new set of business procedures, or figuring out how to program your new phone give you a chance to grow. It's all a matter of how you approach the changes that naturally occur in life.

Just ask my forty-five-year-old banker friend who never envisioned any other career. When he took on his first banking staff work after college, he felt he had signed up for a lifetime. After all, banks may not have paid well, but the work was steady and the profession very secure.

As he climbed the corporate ladder, this banking executive had good assignments, and he loved the business. The banks he worked for were solid and highly respected and the perks were good. His bosses became mentors, and before long he was named a senior vice president. His opportunities had never seemed better. The need to change never entered his mind.

Then something went wrong. Automatic tellers made many branches obsolete. Some real estate loans had gone sour, and two of the bank's competitors went bankrupt. Layoffs were occurring everywhere. The last straw occurred when his own bank was devoured by a regional giant. To justify the purchase price, hundreds of jobs were eliminated, including my friend's. Twenty years down the drain, and no future in the banking business.

And guess what? You could be next.

When two giant New York banks merged, 15,000 jobs were lost overnight. In Colorado, for example, banking jobs declined more than 60 percent in less than three years—all because of bank consolidation and automation. Across the country, something in excess of 100,000 bank jobs have been eliminated—permanently—and the trend continues as huge banks merge. The transition in banking, defense, retailing, communications, just to name a few industries, is major, and it's happening elsewhere too.

Currently, blue-collar jobs are down from 40 percent of the labor force at the end of World War II to 25 percent. Now more than 80 percent of all jobs are in the service and knowledge-related sectors. That means, to be employable, workers will need more education. And there will be far less security on the job as business shifts to meet the demands of new technology, global markets, and intense competition.

It's true that many jobs have been lost, but many more new ones are being added, and they will require new skills. Will you be ready if this trend hits your business? You will if you embrace change as an opportunity rather than as an interruption. To survive, you will need more formal education and training to be prepared for new job specialties. You'll also have to be fast on your feet: on average, young people now entering the workforce will change jobs twelve times during their careers. You may have three or four new careers ahead of you!

Tired of Making Dynamite?

Alfred Nobel, creator of the prestigious Nobel Prize, once woke up to read a notice of his death in the newspaper. It had been a terrible mix-up, but a good one for Nobel. The experience caused him to rethink his life, one that had produced huge profits from the development of dynamite. When he read his own obituary, he realized that he didn't want to be remembered for giving the world the ability to blow itself up. Rather, he wanted a legacy centered on peace, science, and culture. Thus, he funded a wonderful program—the Nobel Prizes—to honor people in these fields. "Every man ought to have the right to prepare a new epitaph midstream in his life," Nobel said.

Put Your Trust in Him

One of the nice things about self-renewal is that we focus on *who* we are rather than on *what* we are. Too often, we derive our identities from the comfortable routine of our jobs and the presumed financial stability of the company we work for. Executives derive phony self-importance from corporate suites, deferential staffs, and superficial publicity. But if you "repot," God may be forcing you to examine yourself away from the trappings of your career. You will identify what really makes you tick,

On the Record

I believe in fixing institutions even when they are not broken— and even before others know that improvements are possible.

I have a desire to make life better and more pleasant for others, to be involved in improving society, and to prepare our institutions for the future.

CHESTERFIELD SMITH
Former president, American Bar Association, Miami, Florida

Being an American, to me, is being close to God. I love this world and always will. I will carry with me, whether I go to heaven or hell, the delight that the Lord allowed me during the course of my life.

I would like to be remembered for being an honest person who tried to do his best and enjoyed life to the fullest.

BARRY GOLDWATER
Phoenix, Arizona
Former U.S. Senator

what gives you value. The result will be a more satisfying life. What counts in the end is not the comfort zone of routine or the temporary rewards of success, but rather the root values that drive your soul.

For those who live modestly, dramatic change seems impossible without risking everything. Most Americans live from month to month, or from paycheck to paycheck. Financially, big moves may be out of the question. Even in those circumstances, there are ways to find new challenges, new beginnings. It is realistic to break bad habits and dull routines. Some changes come in smaller doses, built around the realities of work, family, finances, and established roots. The process starts by facing up to your problems, your boredom, your need for new adventures—however modest.

How do you know if it's time for a change? By listening to that still, small voice of God's Spirit. Somehow, you know in your soul when you need to do something different. You may feel a bit restless or a little depressed. You find yourself complaining about little things. You dread heading off to work a little more than usual. You keep thinking "someday" thoughts:

- Someday I'll quit my job and open a restaurant.
- Someday I'll spend more time with my family.
- Someday I'll go back to school.
- Someday I'll live in a foreign country.

When these signals surface, take the initiative. Accept the fact that it's time to change. Take stock of your life. Set priorities. Make up a dream list. Share it with your family and develop an action plan. Then act.

Steven Covey, in *First Things First*, puts the challenge of making a change this way:

> It takes tremendous courage to be a transition person. It takes courage to be self-honest, to examine your deepest motives and to let go of excuses and rationalizations that keep you from living true to your best self. It takes great courage to realize that you are greater than your moods, greater than your thoughts, and that you can control your moods and thoughts.

During your career there may be times when significant change is impossible. You have responsibilities and you can't walk away from them. But even small changes in your routine can be a form of self-renewal. For example, if you're a golfer, take up a new sport, like tennis, and let your clubs take a break. If you always read books that relate to your career, try reading fiction. Enroll in a personal-enrichment class at a local community college. Volunteer for a new community project. Turn off the television for a week and substitute it with after-dinner conversation with your family.

Suffocated by Boredom?

Returning to California after being away for so long was quite a shock. In contrast to the rapid growth in the area was the shocking sameness of so many of our acquaintances. What's worse is to see the effects of that dull routine on their marriages. An alarming number had been divorced, some after thirty years of marriage. One had dumped two wives during my absence. Another very good friend told me he didn't know what happened to cause his marriage to break up after thirty-two years. "I think the flame just went out," he said. Just like that. How sad. Flames don't go out if you stoke them with renewal.

This particular marriage had been suffocated by boredom and inattention. The couple hadn't created new adventures that would help them grow closer together. Nor had they discussed openly what was bugging them, and what it would take to instill new meaning in their marriage. So they ditched it all, which at the time seemed easier. It never is.

Leaving your hometown and returning years later gives you a unique perspective on others. You see subtle changes your friends miss. For that reason alone, it's good to step back to reflect on your own life. You discover what's missing, and what you'd like to do about it. All that is good for the soul, and for finishing strong in the next chapter of your life.

The Lord of Us All

One thing I have learned in the course of two separate newspaper careers and two more in public service: change made my family stronger, more self-reliant. We learned to love diversity and flexibility, and we gained deep respect for the views of others. We also, I think, became just a little more interesting. One thing is certain, we were working hard to live a full life, and there is no greater sense of joy than that.

It's important to keep yourself open and flexible to new adventures, even those neither planned nor wanted. By fighting inevitable change, you create unnecessary misery and you hinder prospects for success or happiness in the future.

In the end, there is only an end. Each job, each place where we live has a conclusion, no matter how good it was, no matter how successful we are. Power fades. Award plaques rust. New neighbors move in, old ones depart. Only the Lord is above all of this.

You will negotiate the pathway of life far better if you accept change as an adventure rather than an interruption.

Chapter 12

Agelessness

Drink from the Fountain of Youthfulness

I want to be thoroughly used up when I die,
For the harder I work, the more I live.
Life is a sort of splendid torch,
Which I hold for a moment.
And I want to make it burn brightly,
Before I hand it off to future generations.

GEORGE BERNARD SHAW

Faith Keeper

This is the beginning of a new day. God has given me this day to use as I will. I can waste it—or use it for good, but what I do today is important, because I am exchanging a day of my life for it.

When tomorrow comes, this day will be gone forever, leaving in its place something that I have traded for it. I want it to be a gain and not a loss; good and not evil; success and not failure; in order that I shall not regret the price I have paid for it.

DR. HARTSILL WILSON

Do you ever notice how once you reach the ripe young age of, say, forty, you are reluctant to tell people how old you are? Somehow we think forty is old, fifty is ancient, and if you're lucky enough to reach sixty, you're probably flat on your back in a nursing home.

A 180-mile river raft trip down the Colorado River through the Grand Canyon cured me of ever thinking too much about age. We're talking old here. The steep canyon walls on either side exposed some of earth's most ancient geology—granite formations estimated by some geologists to be 2.7 billion years old. Along the way, we also passed some of the oldest traces of human inhabitants in the west—ancient Anasazi hieroglyphics and ruins abandoned more than two thousand years ago. From the ageless perspective of the Grand Canyon, one is overwhelmed by the sense that life is short, and that we must allow what George Bernard Shaw calls "the torch of life" to burn brightly before we hand it off to future generations.

Very few visitors get to see all this splendor from the unique perspective of the river that has been carving the canyon walls for so many years. It's as close as human beings ever get to the center of the earth. From this humbling vantage point, I could not help but appreciate all the good things that have happened in my life and to realize how wrong it is to think of myself as old. Compared to the Grand Canyon, I'm just a kid!

The Long View

Modern culture looks at the immediate, while the true spirit of humanity clings to the eternal. A rich and full life does not measure in terms of hours, days, or years, but in the content of our dreams and how we make them come true. To lead a full life, we need to cherish each day, to embrace the passage of time as a gift to enjoy. Need some examples?

Newspaper columnist Ann Landers has been offering advice to millions of newspaper readers for more than fifty years. At age eighty, she's still writing and keeping up on trends. She's been practical and relevant in her counsel, and universally respected through it all. Will she ever retire? "I plan to die at the typewriter," she says. Ann Landers receives more than a thousand letters a day. Her work keeps her young.

The Lord Has No Retirement Plan

Billy Graham has been preaching to huge audiences for over fifty years. A reporter once asked him when he planned to retire. In characteristic fashion, he replied, "I don't recall seeing the word *retire* in the Bible." I've been privileged to know Dr. Graham as a friend and I can assure you, he'll preach his way right into heaven!

I've known a lot of old people, and most seemed younger than I. I first met Leo Roon when I was in my late twenties and he was in his seventies. Leo was one of those rare individuals who never lost interest in anything, and he did so by staying in touch with young people, the younger the better. He knew what my generation was doing and thinking. Leo believed that there was goodness in everyone. He listened to popular music so that he could understand what kids were thinking, and he wanted to know the latest fads among college students. He cared about politics and the needs of the disadvantaged, and he wanted to contribute in ways that would help improve life for those who would follow his generation. Despite repeated bouts of cancer, he remained as vibrant and alert as a person half his age. Leo Roon, who died at age ninety-three, was a joy to be around because his ageless enthusiasm for life was contagious.

Leo taught me the value of hanging out with people younger than I. If you want to stay young at heart, give it a try. Listen to their crazy ideas (some aren't quite as wild as you might have thought). Listen to their music. Some of it is pretty good, with messages full of thoughtful, positive meaning. Stay in touch with their world because it's your world too. The only way you leave the world of the young is by choice.

I became acquainted with novelist James Michener and his wife, Mari, when they moved to South Florida to write *Caribbean*. I learned that it took Jim many years to discover what he wanted to do with his life. When he did, he started writing books—the first at age forty. From 1947 until his death in 1997, the author published more than fifty best-sellers that have been purchased by over seventy-five million readers.

Not to be outdone by today's computer wizards, Jim turned in his manuscripts not on paper but on computer discs. He kept up with the gadgets of the future. Still writing in his nineties, Jim Michener kept young by reading newspapers, watching television, listening to radio talk shows, and eating at local restaurants.

Shortly after his wife died, I visited this wonderful man at his home near the University of Texas campus in Austin. Despite the loss of his inseparable partner, whom he affectionately called "Cookie," Jim continued to grind it out. I could sense Jim's uncanny resilience and spirit of agelessness. As always, he was as sharp as a tack, with an amazing ability to recall times we had shared together years ago. I asked him how this could be. What made him almost ageless in energy and thought? With quick wit, he responded, "It must be in the genes. But, of course, you can mess it all up with booze and laziness."

> **On the Record**
>
> *My grandmother was an almost perfect role model. She practiced what she preached and lived her life for others. Although she was not a wealthy woman, almost anything she could spare went to ministries at home and missions abroad.*
>
> *When it became necessary for her, in her nineties, to go into a nursing home, she welcomed the opportunity. "There might be some people there who don't know the Lord and I can read the Bible to them."*
>
> ELIZABETH DOLE
> President of the American Red Cross, Washington, D.C.

Another ageless talent is composer and conductor Quincy Jones, who has been in the music business for more than fifty years. Despite his age, Quincy has maintained an amazing ability to keep up with changing musical tastes—from Count Basie to Frank Sinatra to Michael Jackson to Gloria Estefan. "I don't ever want to grow up," Quincy says. "I'm like a child and I always want to be that way. I don't want to be like one of those people who are technically dead inside."

We once had a neighbor, a retired insurance salesman then in his late seventies, who lived for the excitement of Sundays. That was when he picked up people older than he so that they could get to church. Ralph Barnes had a bounce to his walk and an enthusiasm in his voice that stayed with him to the end. I am absolutely convinced that his youthful attitude added years to his life. Rather than feel sorry for himself as an aging widower, he found great joy in helping others.

My good friend Woody Wirt, former editor of *DECISION* magazine, published his twenty-sixth book—at age eighty-five. Most have been about joy; all have been about staying young. One of his titles is a classic: *I Don't Know What Old Is, But Old Is Older than Me.* In two sentences, he has captured the essence of agelessness: "The number one problem with us older people is a lack of vision. We are immortal until the vision fades."

At Fifty, You've Got Thirty More Years!

These days we're living longer, retiring earlier, and remaining healthier. Today, more that 70 percent of all men will reach age sixty-five and, if they do, will live, on average, until eighty-one. An American woman who reaches age fifty without cancer or heart disease will, on average, see her ninety-second birthday. By 2030 there will be an estimated sixty-five million Americans sixty-five or older, or about twice the number as today. Currently, more than fifty thousand Americans have passed age one hundred. These life-expectancy projections make a most important point: on average, we'll live 50 percent longer than our grandparents, but the question is, Will we live those additional years well or will we waste them?

With such prospects for longer, healthier lives come opportunities to plan for and enjoy many years of healthy activity and excitement well beyond what used to be the threshold of normal retirement at age sixty-five. For the first time ever, people over sixty find themselves with increased freedoms and decreased physical limitations.

Author Gail Sheehy, in her book *New Passages*, calls this agelessness phenomenon a "second adulthood—the years after 45 when people run marathons, start new careers, give more of themselves to others, go back to school, learn new hobbies. For many, it's the most rewarding time of life. The kids have been raised, financial security has improved and there is a certain peace that comes from knowing what you realistically can expect to achieve in life."

Sound familiar?

In this world of older demographics, millions face almost another whole life of exciting options after age fifty. The trick is to take advantage of them. The world is changing at a record pace and if we don't keep up with what's new, we'll be left in the dust, choked off from the excitement of new adventures.

Age Beaters

If you're over forty and haven't done the following, you ought to take steps to begin—not because these activities are that important, but because the process of doing them will keep you young.

Learn to use a computer. When I offer this advice to my middle-age friends, they moan, "We'll never make it." Lame excuse—one that will age you premature-ly. It's like ignoring the convenience and essentiality of the automobile when it was introduced in the 1920s. The computer can be the gateway to part-time work, or to fun and games. It can offer everything from continuing education to E-mail communications with the kids and grand-children off in college. The computer is one of the best ways for every-one to stay in touch with the future and, in the process, remain ageless.

Stay in school. Some think that when they finish college, their formal learning is over. All that a university degree assures is access to a permanent state of ignorance, and so continuing education is a critical part of what must become a lifelong search for more knowledge and new challenges. It's all part of that spirit of agelessness.

Stay physically active. The forties are dangerous years in this respect, for that is when we begin to think we are too old to play basketball, swim, ride our bikes, and the like. Once you think old, you act old. Staying physically active, especially in some form of aerobic activity, is not just good for the heart—it's good for the head as well.

Leap across generations. Ever notice how all your friends tend to be your own age? Bad move if you want to have the quality of agelessness. All your conversations focus on pretty much the same things if your social life is confined to your own age group. Be a little more inclusive. Adopt a young couple just starting out, and seek friendships with those who are older.

Climb higher. Faith in God helps me keep an eternal perspective. It makes me realize I am part of something bigger than time. If you have not opened yourself to the possibility of belief in God, I would challenge you to explore this aspect of life. I happen to believe that there is more to life than the seventy or so years each of us is given. Knowing that helps keep me comfortable with whatever age I am and allows me to live each moment to the fullest.

Reach out to others. The best way to stay young is to help someone else. Volunteer to help teach youngsters to read. Deliver meals to senior citizens. Join a local chapter of Habitat for Humanity. Nothing is more exhilarating than seeing others benefit from your input. It elevates your focus away from your own problems and keeps you from the most common symptom of aging: grumbling.

Reshuffle the deck. At each transition in life, take stock of your priorities and adjust accordingly. When Lamar Alexander completed eight years as governor of Tennessee, where there is a two-term limit, he used the transition to take time off with his family. Instead of signing on for big bucks with a local law firm or moving on to a key federal appointment in Washington, Lamar chose to sort out life's priorities by taking his family to Australia. Later he wrote about his experiences in his fascinating book *Six Months Off.* "I realized that back home in America," Lamar wrote, "each of us had been in orbit, a planet in a family solar system, each now and then passing by another family member, close enough to have some sort of relationship but usually glad to speed on past." Not all of us can go to Australia, but we can still rearrange our lives from time to time.

Replace old ruts with new ones. Starting something new contributes to a sense of agelessness. It gives your life a constant sense of "beginning." Never settle for the same old way of doing things, but constantly look to life as an adventure. Special holiday celebrations. A weekly lunch out with your spouse. Family night at the library. Follow your curiosity. Visit new places and make new friends.

Consider age a gift. We have been brainwashed into thinking that age is something to fear. Each year, the limit of what constitutes "old" gets younger and younger. Fight that trend. It is a lie that is spread by the media and popular culture. Your years are like money in the bank—a treasure to be savored and enjoyed. Don't fall for the myth that "you're too old."

Be a little crazy. I also think the spirit of agelessness is fostered by a willingness to try something out of character now and then. Have fun, be a little crazy. As I was

> ## On the Record
>
> *I want to be remembered as a person responsible for the moral and ethical keel of my company. Having become a Christian helped me as a leader understand grace, peace and assurance.*
>
> *As I set the vision for the business, my greatest joy comes from seeing others succeed. It is not what we say in company memos or at the podium that defines our values and assures those around us. It's what we do, day in and day out. And we earn that respect when things are tough, not when they are going well.*
>
> JIM CARREKER
> Chairman and CEO
> Wyndham International and
> Director, Patriot American
> Dallas, Texas

writing this chapter, my daughter Carrie shared with me a wonderful message about shaking loose your "stuffy self." Written by British author Jenny Joseph (and included as the title poem in her best-selling book), the poem reminds us all that the spirit of agelessness is driven by a spirit of new adventure.

When I am an old woman I shall wear purple
With a red hat which doesn't do, and doesn't suit me.

And I shall spend my pension on brandy and summer gloves
And satin sandals, and say we've no money for butter.
I shall sit down on the pavement when I'm tired
And gobble up samples in shops and press alarm bells
And run my stick along the public railings
And make up for the sobriety of my youth.
I shall go out in my slippers in the rain
And pick the flowers in other people's gardens
And learn to spit.

Maybe the best thing you can do to foster your own spirit of agelessness is to just go out in your backyard and practice spitting!

God Loves You—Always

My younger daughter once brought home from a Christian-based summer camp several handwritten pages of beautiful thoughts about life and faith. For years I have cherished my copy of these uplifting messages. One is particularly appropriate when thinking about the remaining years of your life:

Faith Keeper

God loves you just the way you are today, but much too much to let you stay that way.

Chapter 13

Compassion

Gaining from Giving

When I talk to elderly people who are dying, I find they don't worry about material gain or about having too little success in life. They worry about what they should have done with the people they loved.

LEAH DE ROULET

Faith Keeper

It is God himself who has made us what we are and given us new lives from Christ Jesus; and long ages ago he planned that we should spend these lives in helping others.

EPHESIANS 2:10 (TLB)

Dionne Warwick used to sing a great Burt Bacharach tune that went, "What the world needs now is love sweet love, that's the only thing that there's just too little of." It was a very popular melody, and its words rang so true. It made us all feel good, but I can't say that we took her words to heart.

What the world still needs is love. Compassion. Watching out for one another and helping whenever there is need.

Leah de Roulet is a social worker who counsels terminally ill cancer patients and their families. She's seen it all. People close to death have no pretense. They are desperate for love and encouragement, and for understanding about the terror of pain. Leah provides it. It's called compassion.

Compassion is an essential value needed in many circumstances: alongside a hospital bed or with a child as he says his prayers at night. It comes with a warm meal, an open mind, or an outstretched hand. Compassion is expressed with a hug or a phone call. We feel it in church or the doctor's office. Or at least we should. One of the reasons we feel out of sorts as a nation is that sources of compassion seem to have dried up.

But the Greatest of These Is Love

Too often we race through life oblivious to the pain and emptiness in the lives of others we care about, and we do nothing to help. We fail to appreciate that a simple pat on the back can be lifesaving medicine for those in need. Perhaps it's one of your kids who was uncharacteristically quiet. Maybe it's your neighbor whose frown you missed because you were late for work and roared out of the driveway. It might be your widowed mother who hasn't called in a week, or an old college friend whose periodic letter is way overdue.

In the office, you raced off to your next appointment totally unaware that your secretary, who is always cheerful, has deep pain in her eyes. She can't seem to catch your attention long enough to tell you she learned the night before that her husband has lost his job. You're too busy to sense that something is very wrong.

We never fully appreciate the power of compassion in dealing with others. To embrace with compassion someone who is hurting physically or emotionally is to give hope, to show you care, to remind that person that there is love in the world, no matter how tough things get. In such circumstances, your concern means everything to others. But in the process of giving hope and meaning to their lives, you do the same for yourself.

The Power of Human Touch

Phyllis Sippel knows this power of compassion. In the pediatric ward of a New York City hospital where she is an intensive-care nurse, compassion is about all there is to offer a child about to die. I can't imagine tougher duty for anyone. On one occasion, a five-year-old boy with burns over 97 percent of his body was placed under Phyllis's supervision. The child's grandmother claimed that he had been accidentally set afire with a cigarette lighter, but the circumstances seemed very suspect, especially since no one from the family visited the child in the hospital.

The only spot where the boy could be touched without feeling excruciating pain was in a small spot over his right eye. For hours at a time, this caring nurse rubbed this small area as a means of communication. As the boy drifted in and out of consciousness, she read him stories, hoping that the loving tone of her voice might help. She knew the odds were high that this lonely child would not make it, but she was determined to give some comfort for whatever time was left. He died on the twenty-third day, but he had done so wrapped with love and compassion from a caring nurse.

Few of us have such dramatic opportunities to use compassion, but there are many other ways to help. A phone call. Stopping long enough to find out how things are really going with a friend or with someone at work. A simple thank-you to someone who has helped you. A hospital visit. An encouraging word to your children, or to their teachers. It's in the ordinary circumstances of life that compassion can mean the most.

It's been proved scientifically that a hug, or even a brief contact touch through the opening of a preemie incubator, can make a huge difference. One study showed that premature infants who were massaged for fifteen minutes three times a day gained weight 47 percent faster than others who were left alone. "It's amazing how much information is communicated in a touch," one researcher reported. That's why hundreds of hospital volunteers sign up to hold abandoned babies in welfare wards. It also adds poignant meaning to the bumper-sticker question, Have you hugged your child today?

The Lord's Compassion

Some of the most compassionate words I know are offered by Moses in the Old Testament (Numbers 6:24–26):

> The LORD bless you and keep you;
>
> The LORD make His face
>   shine upon you,...
>
> The LORD lift up His
>   countenance upon you,
>
> and give you peace (NKJV).

Compassion can save lives, or make the pain a little more bearable. Compassion soothes the lonely, gives hope to the discouraged, and provides that extra push toward an important goal. Every parent who raises a child must use compassion every day.

On the Record

I would like to be remembered for my Faith in God, Integrity, Concern for the Least, the Last, and the Lost, and for my Patriotism.

My father taught me unselfish love of family and friends and, with eloquent simplicity, he taught me to lead a life of trusting in God—always.

ALVAH H. CHAPMAN, JR.
Former chairman and CEO,
Knight Ridder, Inc.
Miami, Florida

I would like to be remembered for my love of life and my love of God, followed by a sense that we are to treat all individuals on this earth as equals.

DR. PEDRO JOSÉ GREER
Volunteer medical director for Cammilus House, a homeless shelter, Miami, Florida

Going the Extra Mile

Compassionate understanding can require incredible patience and perseverance, especially with those who turn you off. Often those are the very ones who have the most need for compassion. Their ways may be incredibly annoying, but behind it all can be enormous emotional or physical hurt. They need to talk out their problems and they need your encouragement. If you won't help, who will?

That's how Aaron Feuerstein felt just before Christmas in 1995 after a fire destroyed his textile mill outside Boston. More than fourteen hundred employees and their families thought it was all over because the disaster would force Feuerstein to close permanently. Instead, the owner, who had enormous compassion in his soul, announced the day after the disaster that the company would continue to pay the workers until the production lines could be reestablished. It was an unexpected, but crucial, act of compassion. It has also made other corporate barons nervous, worrying that Mr. Feuerstein's example might cause their workers to expect compassion from them.

The toughest work of all involves reaching out to those in deep trouble. What do you say to someone who has just been told she has a month to live? How do you console someone at work who has lost a son in a car accident? How do you deal with your best friend who has lost a spouse or a job? What about a person who is going through a bitter divorce, or the parent whose son has run away, or your neighbor who has just plain given up?

Usually, we avoid these circumstances any way we can. We don't know what to say or do. We're afraid we might be intruding where we shouldn't. Some are too embarrassed to share their problems, but they need someone to provide some encouragement, some reason to hope. Sometimes there is absolutely nothing you can say or do to improve the situation, but your simple presence and willingness to show compassion can be a lifesaver.

Often, just being there for someone and not doing anything else is the most compassionate act you can perform.

Compassion Through Appreciation

Two of the most compassionate words in the English language are "Thank you," and it drives me crazy when people refuse to use them even for the slightest courtesy: a job well done, a service rendered, a door held open, a good meal, a thoughtful comment. Thank-yous convey compassion, and they inspire it in return.

Thanking people at work can be dynamite. It's amazing how many go to work week in and week out and never have any response for their good efforts. It's a terrible environment in a company when staffers have the sense that no one at the top has time to express appreciation down the line where everything gets done. As a publisher, I was always on the lookout for opportunities to thank people for their efforts. A handwritten note from the boss, or better yet a personal visit to the employee's workstation, is often more important than a raise. Well, almost.

Mel Laird, my mentor and boss at the Pentagon, had a great trick when he was a congressman in a mostly rural area of Wisconsin. Whenever he ate out, he always left by way of the kitchen. He simply wanted to thank the cook for the meal. Sure, he picked up a vote or two along the way, but what a wonderful thought. How many times do you think the chef in your favorite restaurant has been thanked for the good meal he prepared?

Try Mel Laird's kitchen tour sometime. While you're at it, why not surprise one of your kids by showing up unexpectedly for that musical performance or basketball game? Stop by and see your friend who is in the hospital, or walk down the street just on the chance that you will run into a neighbor you haven't seen in a while. These are the compassionate things to do, and they count.

When I took over *The Miami Herald*, I made a point of turning the spotlight on people who were generously performing compassionate acts in the city. We stepped up efforts to find those deserving to be uplifted in personal profiles we ran regularly. Our editors and I believed that our newspaper should promote compassion by recognizing it. At the time, compassion was sorely needed in racially divided South Florida—to say nothing of the cocaine trafficking, political corruption, and loss of thousands of jobs as companies went bankrupt or abandoned the area.

In one of my columns in *The Herald,* I featured a six-month-old baby who had been rescued from drug-addicted parents by a local Crisis Nursery. The child had a plate in his head to repair his skull after his parents had intentionally dropped the baby. Thanks to the publicity, the courts speeded up the child's release to adoptive parents, Kathy and Steve Stephen, who have provided the young boy with the compassionate love and stability he desperately needed.

Other columns saluted the work of our South Florida federal judiciary, whose caseload is four times that of the next busiest court in the United States. These dedicated judges needed community support and I tried to help generate it. Unknown to most, I met regularly with the judges over brown-bag lunches to discuss—off the record—how our community could work to meet the need for more jails, prosecutors, and courtroom facilities.

Blessed by an Angel

One of the most amazing stories my column followed centered on Frank and Mary Toro, who have taken in more than a dozen terminally ill children abandoned by destitute parents. Most had lost all hope for survival, that is until they came under this couple's compassionate care.

It all started when the Toros' third child, Teresa, was born with spina bifida, a severely debilitating disease that is often fatal. Rather than feel sorry for their misfortune, the family chose to give this child special compassion—and to take in others who, like her, were severely handicapped or terminally ill. Most had been turned over to the welfare system. One had been abandoned in a cardboard box on an inner-city street. Her name: "unknown white female." Her natural parents couldn't cope.

I'll never forget my first visit to the modest Toro home. It was breakfast time and there were nine mouths to feed. Mary Toro had no time for small talk. "Grab a bottle," she ordered. And so I conducted the interview for my Sunday column while feeding a small, severely handicapped child in my lap. Around me were three very handicapped kids in wheelchairs and four who had to be catheterized every few hours. "I wouldn't trade this for anything," Mary told me. "These children have reinforced my belief that there really is a God."

One of my columns about the Toros generated an anonymous cash gift in excess of $100,000 to help them buy a larger home for their expanded family. It was a gift from heaven, the Toros thought. Tragically, several years later this home was severely damaged by Hurricane Andrew, but the Toros were not to be discouraged. The place has since been fixed up, and their lifesaving efforts, driven by compassion, continue. Every city in America has heroic people like Frank and Mary Toro. The challenge is to find them, and to uplift their examples of compassionate care.

> ## On the Record
>
> *I learned a lot about decency from my father, a Presbyterian minister who treated everyone with tremendous respect. I learned a lot about humor from my mother, who took almost nothing seriously.*
>
> DAVE BARRY
> Columnist and author,
> *The Miami Herald*
>
> *I would like to be remembered for my integrity, my endeavor to always follow the Golden Rule in dealing with others in all conditions and stations in life, and for my service to country, to the Marine Corps, and my community. And, I thank God for his protection in times of danger.*
>
> GENERAL JAMES
> LAWRENCE (USMC Retired)
> Winner of the Navy Cross for
> heroism during the Korean War

We also published extensive feature stories about volunteer organizations that were making a difference in South Florida. Besides giving hope to those working hard on community needs, the coverage also had the effect of encouraging other readers to become involved. On a regular basis, we ran lists of addresses, telephone numbers, and names of contacts so that readers would know how to become involved themselves. We used our editorial pages to salute some of the best work by citizens in our community.

Charitable Americans?

Today, eighty million Americans give their time and talent in support of worthy causes, whether it be down the street or halfway around the world. Most work through caring church groups. They serve food to the homeless, volunteer at hospitals and welfare centers, and sign up to help inner-city church ministries. Others work with handicapped kids, disabled seniors, and the terminally ill. Still others help raise money to conquer cancer, to provide disaster relief, and to feed the hungry. All in the name of compassion.

These people contribute out of the goodness of their hearts, not because they expect to be honored or because they will have a charitable tax deduction. Giving of our time and financial resources is a uniquely American concept. No other country does so much for so many. And much of it is driven by the simple desire to be compassionate.

Many of those who participated in my survey on personal values mentioned that what they were doing for others was as important as what they had done in their careers or for their own families. Their compassion was real. Don Shula has done wonders for United Way, and so have hundreds of pro football superstars who also support this cause. Lockheed Martin's CEO, Norm Augustine, spoke about his work with the Boy Scouts.

TV personality Kathie Lee Gifford told me about the homes she and her husband, sportscaster Frank Gifford, have funded to care for homeless and crack-addicted kids in New York City. Cassidy's Place (named for their daughter) offers programs for poor children who suffer from terminal illnesses. Cody House (named for their son) serves the needs of homeless infants and children. These facilities are part of a network of a dozen homes operated in the New York area by the Association to Benefit Children. Kathie Lee considers her work with indigent kids to be among her most important accomplishments in life. "Being involved with children so different from my own has enlarged my heart and my faith, and it has given me a sense of purpose," she wrote.

Trusting God with Your Life

This talented entertainer talks openly about the importance of her faith and the impact of a Billy Graham crusade on her life. "If there is anything I am tremendously grateful for in my life, it's first that I've known that God loves me and that I have parents who loved me too."

Not everyone can build a home for needy kids or lead a huge community cause, but everyone can reach out and help one person, one modest deed at a time. Through local social-service agencies and churches in your community, you can find dozens of meaningful ways to give compassionate support to those in need.

Speaking of churches, I have a hard time with those places of worship that erect big, new buildings but seldom give anything back to their communities. The Bible teaches the concept of a tithe—a gift of 10 percent of one's income to God. I'd love to see more churches donate a "tithe" of their annual budgets to the communities they serve.

The toughest time of all to be an encourager is when you have few reasons to be encouraged yourself but you know that you have no choice but to uplift those around you. I recall a particularly tough time in Miami when I struggled to write a Sunday column offering encouragement to South Florida's readers a few days after we had been battered by yet another crisis. Miami's inner city had gone up in flames for the third time in as many years. The community was discouraged and terribly divided. I was in no mood to be hopeful as I looked at my blank computer screen, but a messenger of hope I needed to be. Somehow, we as a community had to pick up the pieces. Compassion and encouragement can seem somewhat useless and shallow when hatred and despair are involved, but we had no choice. We needed to tap every ounce of hope from the depths of our soul, and with a little help from above, we did.

Life is often like that. There are times when we must call upon every ounce of optimism and compassion. We need to be encouragers even when there is little reason to be encouraged, and we need to be compassionate even when we're frustrated and angry. Those are the very moments when compassion is needed the most.

Over the years I've collected good advice from others about encouragement. I see it as essential in leading a compassionate life. Here are a few tips.

- Encouragers are compassionate, unselfish, and loving people.
- Encouragers seek out opportunities to help and drop everything for those in need.
- Encouragers count their blessings and help others inventory theirs.
- Encouragers pray for others, and with others.
- Encouragers find the good in others, and they nurture it. No cynics allowed.
- Encouragers forgive and forget, and they listen and observe.
- Encouragers make lists of people to thank and do so. Often.
- Encouragers take advantage of what they have and erase thoughts of what might have been.
- Encouragers can always be counted on.

Brotherly (and Sisterly) Love

Several years ago, my wife and I visited Ephesus, Turkey, where Saint Paul preached in the first century. To walk the marble streets where Paul taught for three years, and to see some of the buildings where his people lived, was absolutely captivating. Paul's *Letter to the Ephesians,* written from prison in Rome, is full of encouragement and compassion. Imagine. Here was a man preaching from jail to his friends in what was then one of the seven major cities in the ancient world. His message was about compassion for his captors and encouragement for his friends. His admonitions have been powerful reminders of my own responsibilities to muster up the same.

Time for Praise and Prayer

There is a wonderful Sunday-morning tradition called Praise and Prayer at the Solana Beach Presbyterian Church near where we live. It's a time in the early-morning service when members of the congregation can stand up and thank God for their blessings and request prayers for those in need.

The diversity of requests is incredible. One Sunday's list was typical. An eleven-week-old baby had barely survived its tenth operation but was not expected to live. An elderly mother had just been informed that her dreaded brain tumor had reappeared. A member's neighbor was killed the day before in an auto accident, and the parents had no religious faith to reassure them. A young college couple stood up to announce their engagement. Another person rose to report that the week before he had lost his job, but he had been comforted by prayer. Another church member talked about the blessings of a new career. One was entering seminary; another had just returned from missionary work in central Mexico. And the final praise: the church truck ministry would be delivering a record amount of food to the needy.

The message from that church congregation was powerful: we care, and we rely upon the Lord for His help. Whenever I hear people speak during this part of the Sunday service, I come away reminded of how much I have to be thankful for in my own life. More important, I am reminded of how much hurt and need there is around me, and how little aware of it I am most of the time.

Do you want to help make this country great again? Find one person, one family, one organization, or one cause. Devote your time, energy, and resources to it for one year. By then, it will become a positive addiction from which you cannot escape.

Chapter 14

Commitment

Nothing Gets Done by Accident

When you are so devoted to doing what is right that you press straight on and disregard what men are saying about you, there is the triumph of moral courage.

PHILLIPS BROOKS

Faith Keeper

Subordinate yourself to a higher calling: your family, your church, your business, your nation, and there will always be fulfillment.

My involvement with employees cannot be limited to a transaction of wages paid for work done. Since each person has been created in God's image and has a unique value and worth, I must take the time to understand, to love, and to serve that person with the clear objective of having the work environment become a positive influence.

TOM PHILLIPS
Former chairman and CEO,
Raytheon Corporation

It was almost dark when we drove up to a busy corner in Miami's Liberty City to buy cocaine, and I was amazed how easy it was. A half-dozen pushers stood around hawking marijuana and crack, so popular that it was sold by brand names. Ain't No Secret and Top Choice were among the best, I was told, because they packed the most "high" for the buck. Nearby, from the safety of their apartments, the neighbors watched as dozens came by for their illegal fix.

Some were on foot, others drove beat-up cars, and a few came by in very expensive sports models. There were lawyers, fourteen-year-old girls, mechanics, well-dressed businessmen, and a newspaper publisher in jeans and baseball cap. Cocaine knows no class.

And then, the surprise came. Accompanying me were well-disguised undercover agents whose tactics were to buy cocaine from the dealers, arrest them, and then take over the corner. From there, the agents spent the rest of the night peddling cocaine to unsuspecting customers who, in turn, were arrested and hauled off to jail. It was a reverse sting operation that led hundreds of unsuspecting cocaine buyers into a trap set by the police who were posing as drug dealers.

I accompanied the police because I wanted to understand the drug scene up close. For six hours I watched the same sequence over and over again. The driver asked for some crack, money changed hands, and the arrest was made. A few tried to escape but were cut off by patrol cars down the street. One pulled a gun, but no one was hurt. Another had to be wrestled to the ground as the officers tried to handcuff him, but the culprit was quickly subdued. Many dissolved in tears. My guess is that they were casual users who would now have to confess their addiction to family and employers.

Before that night's operation was over, 250 had been booked in a processing site nearby, taken to jail, and required to post a stiff bond the next morning. Many, unfortunately, would be back out on the streets buying cocaine again. It was a vicious circle. It also was a frightening scene.

These undercover agents put their lives on the line every time they showed up in that neighborhood. Lose their cover and they could be dead within twenty-four hours. It was scary work, but they did it for one reason: they were committed to a cause.

As head of *The Herald*, I wanted to try to understand the dynamics of our troubled city. In my opinion, it's a newspaper's sacred responsibility to celebrate the goodness of its community, and it was in that spirit that I rode ambulances with paramedics racing to the aid of shooting victims, spoke with cocaine-addicted prostitutes who roam the downtown streets, watched tears flow from the eyes of abused and abandoned kids, and ate with the homeless. I visited hospitals, talked with doctors and professors, and worked to promote the needs of business. I spoke in synagogues and churches to Jews, Protestants, Catholics, and black fundamentalists, and tried out my Spanish at mass in Little Havana.

Everywhere I went, I found unselfish people who had dedicated their lives to helping others. For them, life's meaning came from the commitment. There are hundreds of similar people in your neighborhood too, and you can join their cause.

Walking the Talk

There's no shortage of people willing to talk about the need for change. Just listen to any campaign speech. But where the rubber meets the road is in their commitment to do more than talk. Anyone can talk about making America better. I'd rather "listen" to action.

Commitment to goals, to yourself, and to others is pivotal to making this country great again. It involves much more than showing up or simply carrying out a task with little enthusiasm. To be committed is to have a passion, an ultimate loyalty to something you really believe in. These officers on the front line of crime in the inner city had committed themselves to a cause they felt strongly about, and they carried it out with a mix of passion and incredible bravery. All those people in Miami who were trying to help those trapped in poverty and violence had made a commitment to making life better. That's what will ultimately put our nation back on track.

Isn't it amazing how a committed life can inspire you to greater courage? A young woman studies to be a nurse because she wants to commit her life to helping others. A teenager commits his energy to being the best athlete possible so that he can earn an athletic scholarship, thus using sports as a means of funding the college education he would not otherwise have. A young minister decides to become a missionary abroad and commits his life to doing so. When I hear those stories, my hope is rekindled and my own commitment strengthened. I would love to see a wildfire of commitment break out in this great country.

I don't think it is just a coincidence that so many who responded to my "On the Record" survey used the word *commitment* to describe their lives and what they learned from parents and mentors. Commitment to work. To human needs. To family and friends. To country and religious faith. Commitment seems to be the common denominator of greatness. I think that's because our lives aren't worth much without believing in causes and the people we care about.

Foundational Commitments

Two of the most important commitments we make in life are to God and to another person through marriage. Despite some who have not yet been able to honestly say they believe in God, the core of our nation is composed of those who have given their lives to their Lord, and they work hard to live up to His expectations. Unfortunately, we have allowed our media and some in our government to make us feel as if commitment to God is unimportant—or at least so private that no one should ever find out about our beliefs. And yet, in times of trouble, we turn to God. Our true commitments are most visible in the face of crisis.

Teaching Our Children to Honor God

I am sad to say that it is in the area of marriage that commitment seems to have lost some ground. Having come from a "broken" home, I understand the pain of divorce and in no way want to increase that pain for any whose marriages have deteriorated. I realize that at one time most married people were committed to a long and joyful marriage, and like you, I grieve over the soaring divorce statistics. But I also have to celebrate the fact that more than half the marriages today do last. Husbands and wives commit to each other, and through the best of times and the worst, they hang in there. Because they believe in living up to their commitments, they work out their differences, and their relationship grows.

If we could only teach our children to honor God and enter their marriages as lifelong commitments, I truly believe most of our nation's social problems would eventually disappear.

Strengthened by Fire

Some commitments are nurtured when people have hit bottom. Anwar Sadat, former president of Egypt, spent six years of his life in jail as a political prisoner. It was then that he strengthened his love for his countrymen and his faith. "It was through suffering that I discovered how I was by nature inclined to do good, that love was the real motivation behind my action," he wrote in his autobiography. Chuck Colson, sent to prison during Watergate, has told how prison shaped his commitments too: "It was there that I discovered that the object of life is not prosperity, as we are made to believe, but the maturing of the soul." Since then Chuck has used the power of that commitment founded on his beliefs as a Christian to give hope to thousands of prisoners and parolees around the world.

When San Francisco Forty-Niner fullback William Floyd wrecked his knee halfway through the 1995 season, he never gave up. Instead of feeling sorry for himself and staying home until he recovered, he stood on the sidelines at every workout so that he could inspire his teammates with enthusiasm and optimism. Floyd had made a pledge to his team and he wasn't about to walk away from it, even though he knew he would be out for the season. At the end of the year, his teammates voted him the player "who best exemplifies inspirational and courageous play." William Floyd taught the players and fans what commitment is all about.

You may be going through a difficult time right now, perhaps wondering why it had to happen to you. Believe me, I know this is tough advice to swallow, but can you at least entertain the possibility that what you are going through is making you a better person? Can you use this time to reexamine your commitments and emerge stronger? As I look back on my life, I see those trials as milestones of growth. They helped me identify what was really important in life and strengthened my commitment to those things. While I was in the crucible, however, it didn't feel like good medicine. Try to envision yourself on the other side of your dark valley and let that good view encourage you to hang on.

> ### On the Record
>
> *One of my most important accomplishments was ending America's involvement in Vietnam while at the same time ending the draft and developing the All-Volunteer service.*
>
> MEL LAIRD
> Former Secretary of Defense
> Senior Counselor, *Reader's Digest*
>
> *My friend, David Williams, showed me optimism, enthusiasm, and infectious goodwill under the most trying conditions as we spent about one and a half years together in a German POW camp in World War II. He was totally dedicated to the well-being of others.*
>
> BARRY SHILLITO
> Former Assistant Secretary of
> Defense, San Diego, California

One of the things I admire most about Ronald Reagan is that he never waffled. Whether they agreed or not, the voters knew where Reagan stood. The core of his beliefs centered on a strong defense, lower taxes, and less government, and he never wavered from those commitments during the sixteen years he served as governor of California and president of the United States. I think even his opponents respected him, and in a day when so many political leaders break their promises almost daily, we yearn for a leader with the commitment of a Ronald Reagan.

Commitment Is a Choice

Some of my most important commitments were made when I was a teenager living in a rather modest neighborhood in Queens, New York. My parents were divorced just as I started high school at age fourteen, at a time when people simply didn't talk about splitting up. As I looked at my own future, there seemed to be absolutely no way I could afford a good college education. It was a scary time in my life.

Under the circumstances, I had one choice: to work very, very hard. And I did, washing windows in our row-house complex, driving a garbage truck in the summer, and working on a house-wrecking crew in Manhattan. At two bucks an hour, funding college education was a distant dream, but I was determined to get ahead and knew that I would need to do it on my own.

My dilemma was not unique in those days. Nor is it today. Thousands of good people work hard and move ahead, inspired by good people, loving parents, and the multitude of educational options out there. My first major commitment would be to get through college. The second, even more important to me at that time, was to do well enough in life that my children would never, ever have to worry about whether college was available to them—provided, of course, that they were up to the challenge and willing to work for it. They too would have to make commitments.

My wife and I lived up to that pledge together, seeking out good education for our three children. They learned early that hard work was important, and we tried to encourage them every step of the way. When our last child walked onto the stage to receive her college degree, it was a moment to savor; I had lived up to a commitment made forty-two years earlier. It didn't take much for my family to understand why it was such a deeply moving moment for me. With three children now out of college, and one having graduated from law school, I had fulfilled a goal that meant more to me than words could express. It was a defining commitment in my life.

During those high-school years in New York, we lived week to week. The war had just ended and tremendous upheaval was occurring everywhere. Jobs were not easy to find, and I wondered whether I'd ever amount to anything. I had no choice but to believe in myself. I needed to generate an attitude of hope and enthusiasm even when I had little reason for either. But Someone was looking out for me, and that led to another commitment.

An Answer to Prayer

April 3, 1953, is a date I'll never forget. It was then that I learned I had won a Navy ROTC scholarship. With it, my entire college education, including tuition, room, and board, was assured, all in exchange for three years of active duty following graduation. It was a small price to pay.

To this day, April 3 is my own private holiday. It's a commitment, if you will, because each year I pause to thank God for providing one of the greatest breaks in my life. Thanks to answered prayer and the United States Navy, doors of opportunity had miraculously opened. The American Dream was alive and well in my life. It was an important affirmation of my belief that if you commit to hard work, you can be rewarded for it.

We all have events like these that define our futures. I call them thresholds. These are the times when we set goals and make commitments to achieve them. They become the measures, like benchmarks, against which we can compare how far we have come.

On the Record

I have had many mentors. One was devoted to helping those around him move ahead. Another demonstrated the value of a positive, constructive attitude, and the third mentors were my father and mother, who did it all.

NORMAN AUGUSTINE
President and CEO,
Lockheed Martin
Bethesda, Maryland

I believe that integrity is non-negotiable, loyalty is a two-way street, and disagreement is not disrespect.

GENERAL JULIUS BECTON
(U.S. Army—Retired)
Former president,
Prairie View A&M University

Commitment and the courage of conviction are values that extend beyond material success.

DAVID McLAUGHLIN
President, The Aspen Institute
Former president,
Dartmouth College

All of us can remember when we bought our first car on time because we barely had enough for a down payment. Couples remember their first, heavily mortgaged home or the hand-me-down furniture that we used in our first apartments. We barely made enough to get by, but somehow we did, and now we look back on it all with amusement—but also a little pride. After all, we had committed to get ahead and we had done so, even if that process only means that we have bigger homes and larger mortgages.

But commitment isn't something you do just in your earlier years. It is a process that involves constant attention. I'm convinced that most marriages that fail do so not because there was never a commitment, but because that commitment was neglected. You need to "feed" your commitment, pay attention to it, remind yourself of it. Instead, we make a commitment to something, then go on autopilot. That simply doesn't work.

When my military duty ended in Washington in 1960, I decided to move west. Ever since my destroyer duty in the Pacific, California had been burned into my soul. So with all my worldly possessions packed in the trunk of my car—and room to spare—I drove across country, unemployed and with only enough cash for gas and cheap motel rooms along the way. By the time I reached San Diego, my cash reserves had dropped to seventy-five dollars and there was no job in sight.

There I was, broke and unemployed, with a terrific liberal arts education that had prepared me for the world, but not for work. Talk about a humble moment. It was a personal threshold I'd never forget . . . and it was a time to turn to prayer.

Soon after arriving, I landed a job keeping retirement records for the Copley group of newspapers, whose flagship was the *San Diego Union-Tribune*. Therein began my newspaper career—totally by chance. By the mid-1960s I had moved up the ranks in the newspaper world, but my passion for optimism was severely tested as I watched our country being torn apart by civil riots at home and a divisive war abroad. It was popular then to tear down America, but I found that negative perspective unacceptable. So I took a different route—speaking and writing about positive trends and the need to be optimistic. Many who heard or read my message saw absolutely nothing to be optimistic about. I didn't care because I thought they were wrong.

I sometimes wonder where I would be today if I had not remained committed to putting my education to work and standing firm on my refusal to be negative.

Take Stock

Look back on your own life. Were there thresholds where you had to take a stand? Was your commitment what it should have been? Is it today? The nice thing about commitment is that it can be renewed. Maybe you need to set some time aside to think back on the commitments you have made and ask yourself these three questions:

- Am I still committed to that idea or person?
- How would my life be different if I gave up on that commitment?
- What do I need to do to strengthen that commitment?

As you examine your commitments, ask yourself, What are the priorities of my life and how do I achieve them? What is the most meaningful, and how do I build those experiences into my routine?

There's no better definition of the power of commitment.

One Priest's Humble Calling

One of the most committed men I have ever met was Monsignor Marc Taxonera, a Benedictine monk at the Montserrat Monastery located in the saw-toothed mountains twenty miles west of Barcelona. This humble priest has committed his entire life to two causes: prayer and the care of a collection of books that date back to the twelfth century. Some of the rare books, hand-lettered and beautifully illustrated, represented a lifetime of work for one monk. It became his lifelong commitment to preserve them safely in a remote, sixth-floor library of this famous sanctuary. He's done this for fifty-one years.

Is there anything you could dutifully commit yourself to for so long? A few weeks later I had occasion to travel to Valencia, east of the monastery on the east coast of Spain. It was there that I met José Lladro, who with his two brothers founded a factory known around the world for its beautiful porcelain statues. The Lladro brothers are committed to two goals. The first is excellence. The brothers have worked hard to maintain the highest quality in their products, and they have succeeded. Today the Lladro name represents the finest in porcelain craftware.

The Lladro brothers are deeply committed to their people too. Their place is not a factory; it's called the House of Artists, a place where two thousand artisans work as a family. Long before American industry made the human needs of its workers a priority, Lladro built free health clinics and day-care centers. And each day it sends buses around town to pick up wheelchair-bound employees, many of whom are among the best creators on the staff. With commitment and encouragement, these workers produce ceramics that are admired around the world.

The world is full of dedicated people whose lifework centers on producing quality products and serving the needs of others. They maintain high academic standards, achieve superior performance in sports, teach well, and raise good kids. Each is driven by a personal decision to be her best, and each has a constant commitment to remain his best. You can too.

Hard work and flexibility are absolutely essential to survive in today's stripped-down workplace. There are no free rides anymore. No assured job security either. Those who commit to giving their work everything they have, and to learning quickly along the way, are far more likely to get ahead.

Live Your Faith in the Secular World

The companies where we work must share in those commitments too. Many corporations today have goals and mission statements dealing with customers, employees, and shareholders. Such words as *trust, quality, reliability,* and *integrity* appear in these statements over and over again. These are the commitments that describe successful businesses today. But they need to be more than mere words. They need to be lived out daily by everyone from the CEO on down.

In my opinion, it is commitment that drives the network of community agencies that help out in times of need. Thanks to contributions from thousands of Americans, the American Red Cross responds to some sixty thousand disasters each year. The Boy Scouts and Girl Scouts train and guide hundreds of thousands of young people. The Salvation Army runs six thousand facilities, from drug and alcohol rehabilitation centers to group homes for unwed mothers. The United Way campaign supports hundreds of local social-service agencies, while local Boys and Girls Clubs provide healthy activities for kids who otherwise would likely end up troublemakers. Second Harvest operates a national network of 185 food banks that feed twenty-six million people a year. More than fourteen million took advantage of YMCA programs, and Goodwill Industries staffs fourteen hundred thrift stores while training more than 100,000 job seekers, thus moving them from welfare to paychecks.

As you evaluate your own commitments, keep these ideas in mind:

- Commitments need to be carefully thought out. Once in place, they must be lived up to.
- Commitments require that you stick to principle.
- Commitments can best be carried out in an atmosphere of mutual respect.
- Commitments help define the goals of your life, and they become the impetus for getting there.
- Commitments shape your work, embrace your family, and enhance your career.
- Commitments inspire your best efforts. They set an example. They define your legacy.

The Power of a Simple "Thank You"

Years ago Mother Teresa told the story of a woman who had died in her arms. This simple Albanian nun's presence alone had made it possible for a dying human being to leave this earth with a sense of worth. Her last words were "Thank you." No bitterness. No hatred or resentment. Just gratitude. All because of the humble power of faith and prayer from a humble woman who committed her life to serving the untouchables.

The late industrialist Armand Hammer once said:

> *I believe we are here to do good. It is the responsibility of every human being to aspire to do something worthwhile, to make this world a better place than the one we found.*

In recent months, no one exhibited this key principle better than Erika Knight Fox, a talented and dedicated bilingual elementary school teacher who was diagnosed with cancer in her late twenties. Rather than give up, Erika, my daughter Kelly's college roommate and close friend, accelerated her commitment to make the world a better place. Even as she battled this horrible disease and suffered multiple rounds of massive chemotherapy, she devoted her fading energies to writing a book designed to help Hispanic kids who have cancer.

In March 1998 things got grim for Erika and several weeks later she wrote a moving message for worldwide Cancer Prayer Day:

> *I have been dealing with cancer for more than two years. The doctors told me that there was nothing more to be done for me but to keep me comfortable. We decided to turn the chemotherapy off.*
>
> *I was at peace because I was in God's hands. To know that so many people have been praying for me has put me at peace. I think that it was when I put my trust in God that I began to get better.*
>
> *I thank God for each new day He gives me. It is like a gift or a bonus. Now, I have a feeling of confidence because I know that whatever happens, it is the best for me.*

Erika died five days later but she knew that she was at peace; at peace with God and with a loving family and close friends who had been at her side every step of the way. In the end, she found ultimate comfort in the knowledge that she truly had made the world a better place.

You can too.

Chapter 15

Family

"Parent" Is a Verb

*My mother never lost faith in me. She taught
me right from wrong, and she encouraged
me to think and act with an open mind and,
hopefully, with regard to the feelings and
beliefs of others.*

ARTHUR SULZBERGER
Chairman and CEO, *New York Times*

Faith Keeper

*The greatest gift you can ever
receive is to know that you are
loved by God, by your family and
by your friends.*

REV. ERNEST LEWIS

"**F**amily values" are in. But if you think family values are the domain of a particular political party or special-interest group, you're wrong. The American family is at risk, and it is in everyone's best interest that we do our best to reduce the risks.

Without the stability of family, nothing works. That's why, in my opinion, we are having so many problems in our country today. You know the statistics, so I won't belabor them, but a few are chilling reminders of what we are up against.

- Almost 50 percent of all marriages end in divorce. Every year more than a million children are victims of divorce.
- On any given day, about 40 percent of all children in America will go to sleep at night in a home where their father does not live.
- Kids whose parents are divorced are twice as likely to drop out of high school, and they'll be poorer too. Children in fatherless homes are far more likely to grow up poor, to have problems in school, and to get into trouble with the law.
- Of every hundred children born today, twenty-five will be born out of wedlock, and only forty-one will reach age eighteen having lived continuously with both parents. In the inner city, a huge majority of kids don't even know who their father is. At the rate we are going, one out of every two children may be born out of wedlock early in the next century.
- When both parents are working, children spend an average of only seventeen hours a week with their parents. Filling the void is television, watched by children ages six to twelve an average of four hours a day. By age eighteen, kids will have spent more time watching television than sitting in the classroom.

Added to the above, of course, are the problems of child abuse, domestic violence, drugs, teenage crime, and an economy that makes it increasingly impossible for a family to get by without both parents working.

Start in Your Own Home

I don't know about you, but whenever I read the litany of agony afflicting the institution of family, my first reaction is to throw up my hands in despair. What in the world can anyone do to reverse these horrible trends? Well, as with most everything else in life, it must start with one parent, one child, one family at a time. There's no other way.

A stable family is fundamental to our way of life — our values, our system of justice, our sense of human dignity. Yet it seems to be the area where we are most impatient. If things don't work out, we give up without even trying. No-fault divorces and prenuptial contracts make it too easy to discard it all. Even the best of marriages take work and constant renewal. One person speculated that we really need to get married to each other every five years because we change so much in the interim.

Family life takes time too. Husbands and wives need to spend more time with each other. They need to be more sensitive to problems so that they can be talked out early, well before they become crises. In homes where both are working, they need to set aside quality time away from work and away from chores at home. When children are involved, the need for family time becomes even more important.

Families involve single people too. Many prefer to remain single, and have their own special needs for the strength of family. Many of those who are divorced need family to recover. Some will choose to remain single but also need their families. What's important is that there be family support networks to help sustain us all, through the good times and the bad.

When family problems arise today, the good news is that there is more help out there than ever before — professional counseling, divorce recovery groups, self-esteem programs to lift up the spirits of those who have failed along the way. Just the openness with which family issues are discussed is therapy in and of itself.

Above all, there is a huge outpouring of commitment to restoring fundamental family values. Major studies and conferences have focused on family issues. Church groups have made family issues their focus, and hundreds of excellent, practical books are available to help nurture the family and to deal with potential problems early on. A national political debate has centered on family issues too, and that's all very healthy.

As Senator Sam Nunn put it in my survey: "Each American must be taught that to bring a child into the world involves taking responsibility for what happens to that child. This is a battle that must be won one child at a time. I am optimistic that it can be won because of the millions of Americans, young and old, who volunteer their time to improve conditions in their communities, helping others on a one-to-one basis." Think of how much progress we'd make if every adult who is surrounded by love and a stable family took the time to reach out to help create a similar environment for just one other person. What a terrific change we'd see!

Everyone Deserves a Family

This brings me to another point, and that is the matter of the extended family. Where there is no family stability, we must create substitutes. There are several ways to do so:

- We must uplift family responsibility—and there is an enormous desire to do this. That's why a million black men and their sons marched on Washington. That's why PromiseKeepers has filled almost one hundred stadiums with over a million fathers who were there to honor their Christian-

On the Record

My Dad, by example, taught us to work hard and to think of others. George's mother always looked for the good in others. George Bush taught me that if you try your hardest, are decent and honest, you can do anything you want.

BARBARA BUSH
Houston, Texas

My mother was more of a peacemaker, while Daddy was more of a change-maker. My mother was the essence of a great teacher, a loving mother, and a caring soul. My daddy was more of a go-out-and-change-the-community person. He fought for farmers.

GOVERNOR JIM HUNT
Democrat, North Carolina
Raleigh, North Carolina

My mother taught me to work hard and do right. Her personal example of unqualified love gave me the solid foundation of my life.

TOM JOHNSON
President, CNN
Atlanta, Georgia

based commitments as fathers, husbands, and sons.

- A recent CNN poll reported that 80 percent of all parents feel guilty about not spending enough time with their children. As families, we need to spend more time together. Around the dinner table. At night, helping with homework. On weekends, with fun activities.

- Neighbors need to help neighbors. Too often we ignore cries for help when they are just down the street. Often a neighbor is the first to sense that something's terribly wrong next door—an abused child, a battered wife.

- Adopting kids without homes is important too. At any given moment there are twenty thousand children free to be adopted but languishing in government care. They need homes, and there are thousands out there who can't have children or who would welcome the chance to bring a needy one into their family.

- Churches need to become more involved in the inner city. Too many congregations fled to the suburbs years ago and spend time sending missionaries halfway around the world when they should also be working at home.

- We need strong leadership in our schools so that the principal and teachers can become role models. And parents from functioning families need to spend more time helping those schools. In many instances, the only place where kids can learn values is at school. If we fail them there, we've lost them forever.

- Businesses and community organizations need to sponsor schools and neighborhood after-school programs. They need to encourage more involvement by their employees and uplift those who do help.

- As federal spending is cut and programs once funded at the national level are returned to the states and cities, we'll need volunteer leadership more than ever to help the thousands of nonprofit, local programs that provide care and relief to those who have never experienced family love.

Preserving the Family

In my lifetime, I doubt that we will make significant progress in lowering the divorce rate, but we can make a dent. First, I think more and more young people have come to realize that divorce is devastating, not just to themselves but to their children and their extended families.

It may surprise you to know that there are aspects of Bill Clinton's background that this Republican relates to—and respects—in a very personal way. Both of us had a burning determination to overcome the trauma of a broken home. Both of us had hard-working, divorced mothers who were strong and positive influences in our lives.

I agree with columnist and author Michael J. McManus, who would like to see every church require premarital counseling before allowing couples to be married. He calls churches "blessing machines," in that they perform thousands of ceremonies but do not play an active role in supporting the unions they have blessed.

Renewing Our Vows Before God

In 1987, when Joan and I celebrated our twenty-fifth wedding anniversary, we renewed our marriage vows in church. It was a wonderful moment of recommitment. With only our pastor and three children present, we recited the oath we had taken before family, friends, and our

On the Record

I have four children by my late wife and two brought into our family by my present wife. All are individuals of faith, character, and integrity. I can call each my best friend.

WILLIAM BROCK
Former U.S. senator, Republican,
Tennessee, Washington, D.C.

My mother instilled love, family, integrity, good manners, respect for others, high ethical standards, and responsible judgment. My stepfather—Gerald R. Ford— instilled love, family, integrity, fair play, ambition, common sense, and community service.

FORMER PRESIDENT
GERALD FORD
Rancho Mirage, California

My mother and wife built their lives on a rock solid foundation of integrity. Innate kindness and respect for others characterized their daily lives.

DONALD PETERSEN
Former chairman and CEO,
Ford Motor Company

Lord years earlier. Before we did so, each of us spoke briefly about our love and family. Joan had captured the meaning of it all:

Faith Keeper

Marital success is a choice. In these days of contracts and legalism, we have chosen a different course. We have chosen to make a covenant with each other and with our Lord. A covenant is a promise binding two parties, an unconditional commitment.

In the last few years I have felt the presence of Jesus Christ in my life and in our marriage more than ever before. His presence has made a difference to me. There is more love, more patience and a different perspective.

You may not have the best marriage, and your family may be struggling a bit. But take heart. Never give up. You're working at it. You've decided to keep trying, and that, above all, is the best way to strengthen our nation's "family values." No law, no federal policy, no church marriage rule will do as much as your own single-minded determination to make it work.

Syndicated newspaper columnist Ellen Goodman puts the good news this way: "I'm hardly a pollyanna about family life. I know the stress of the sandwich generation, trying to be all things to all bosses, parents, children, spouses. I know every family has troubles. At some time or other, we all look dysfunctional. But the fact is that most of us are functioning. And loving."

I find that wonderfully comforting, don't you?

Chapter 16

Community

Venture Out of the Cocoon

All values are important, everyone who has ever touched my life in some way was a mentor for good or bad. Life is a blend, and a person is a blend of all the influences that have touched their lives.

GENERAL COLIN POWELL
Former chairman, Joint Chiefs of Staff

Faith Keeper

What a wonderful God we have — he is the Father of our Lord Jesus Christ, the source of every mercy, and the one who so wonderfully comforts and strengthens us in our hardships and trials.

And why does he do this? So that when others are troubled, needing our sympathy and encouragement, we can pass on to them this same help and comfort God has given us.

2 CORINTHIANS 1:3–4 (TLB)

How did you become the person you are? What contributed to your personality, your beliefs, your values? If you think you have arrived at your current destination "on your own," you are sadly mistaken. You are also a very sad person, because you have not acknowledged the joyous truth of human development. As Colin Powell reminds us, we are all a part of a greater entity known as community.

Your most important values are molded by others: a loving family, compassionate neighbors, ethical workplaces, and an uplifting church life. All those things together we call community. Each experience, good and bad, flows from this network of influence. For better or worse, these communities of family, friends, neighbors, and work colleagues help make us who we are.

I have often asked what has made me the way I am. Who has most influenced my life? These are great questions for you to consider as well, because a special joy comes from reflecting on those who have meant the most to you. Take some time now to try to name at least seven people who have had an influence on you, followed by a specific contribution they made in your life.

The Importance of Mentors

In my case, it was my mother, who as a single parent raising two boys on a modest secretary's salary, taught me about hard work and perseverance. Ed Heiser, my college roommate and friend for over forty years, has reminded me of the importance of special memories and unquestioned loyalty to those you care about. Then came Mel Laird, who showed me the power of effective communications, and Alvah Chapman, who exemplified commitment and integrity. And, above all, my values have been nurtured by Joan and our children, who have shown me how to be more accepting and less judgmental, and how to balance hard work with the simple blessings of life. To round out this admittedly incomplete list, I would add our longtime pastor, Dan Yeary, who nurtured my faith in

God and my understanding of His Word through the Bible.

None of these influences happened in a vacuum. I met these people in community. They, at various times in my life, were part of a nurturing group of people who taught me things I could not have learned as effectively elsewhere. Do you think your children will have the same opportunities to grow through your community? Or have our communities become closed off by fear and intolerance?

Hiding in Our Cocoons

In my opinion, one of the main reasons that our values system has crumbled in America is because our communities are falling apart. Look at your own community. How often do you get together just for the fun of it? How much neighborly time is spent on our front porches? Rather than sharing together, our homes have become private escapes, giving way to what some call "cocooning"—shutting ourselves inside to enjoy the creature comforts. But in the process, we are missing out on the benefits of learning and growing from one another.

A key part of nurturing the concept of community involves accepting diversity as a natural, inevitable part of life. Diversity should be celebrated, not feared—yet it isn't. Today, our communities are full of bigotry and hatred. We are more divided than ever, with a new wave of racism spreading across the country.

God's Universal Language

What a shame, because there is so much to be gained when we share our lives with others. In South Florida, I was a member of Miami's smallest minority—a white "Anglo," the label for anyone of any ethnic group who wasn't black, Jewish, or Hispanic. My perspective there gave me convincing evidence of the wonderful benefits of diversity. I ate soul food with blacks and prayed in Spanish with Cubans. We celebrated with Jewish friends on their high holy days, and we prayed with Southern Baptists.

Sadly, too many see diversity as a threat when it needs to become synonymous with inclusiveness. We need to change because the world of many languages, cultures, and traditions is real for our children. Most will not be able to get along without understanding this exciting new opportunity. If we and our children fail to adjust, we will drive crippling wedges within our communities and everyone will lose out. We must not let this happen. After all, except for American Indians, we are all immigrants to this land.

No matter how honorable our values in life might be, they are worth very little if our communities are isolated pockets of like-minded people. Neighborhood crime is not someone else's problem; it's ours. If Congress continues to spend more than it takes in, that affects the value of your savings. If the largest employer in town can't compete, it's your job that is at stake. If our streets are unsafe, if our schools can't educate, if our inner cities are exploding with violence, everyone pays the price.

Like it or not, our communities are the sum total of the best and the worst in each of us—from inspiring churches to ugly slums, from honor roll students to dropouts, from unselfish volunteers to vicious criminals. Newspapers have a key role in reporting all this—the good and the bad. But they also have a duty to uplift our communities. Without that encouragement, communities—just like people—give up and die. That means your newspaper must be passionate in balancing the inevitable hard news with feature stories that give people hope.

My Knight Ridder colleague Rolfe Neill, former publisher of the *Charlotte Observer*, was absolutely on target when he said:

> *Newspapers are preoccupied with the auditing function. You can audit your communities but it needs to be done in*

On the Record

My best advice came from a friend immediately after I was named to a top county job: "Son, in this job you will have millions of opportunities to keep your mouth shut. Take advantage of all of them."

DEWEY KNIGHT
Former assistant county manager
Dade County, Florida

There are only two types of humans—negative and positive. I determined to always be positive.

CONGRESSMAN
DANTE FASCELL
Miami, Florida

a sort of motherly fashion. You can audit your children, but
they need to know they will be loved, nurtured, and guided.
A newspaper should not be afraid to put its arms around a
community and say, 'I love you.'

Some big-city editors don't like that concept, but I guarantee that
when a community is in trouble, the newspaper is too.

My guess is that every generation, at one time or another, has felt that
America was going to hell. Ours is no exception. For some time we have
been convinced of this downhill slide, believing that there was no way
the situation would improve. Let's not forget, though, that there have
been many times when our country was in bad shape, but with the help
of God and in the uniquely American tradition, we have always shown
resilience and the ability to renew ourselves. We can do it now!

Restoring American Communities

The first thing we can do to bring a sense of community back is to participate. Sounds easy enough, but we aren't doing enough of it. Every
week, something worthwhile and edifying is happening in your community. It may be a high-school band concert, a church picnic, a soft-
ball game, or a town meeting. In most cases, organizers of such events
will tell you they always have lots of empty seats. What a shame, because
these types of activities really build community.

How long has it been since you attended a school-board meeting (or
have you ever)? Between the local school board and your township government, an awful lot of community-related decisions are made. Are
you there to make sure your voice and views are heard? Do your children's teachers and principals know you? You will never enjoy the benefits of community if you don't participate.

On a more political level, we would go a long way toward restoring
community by returning failed federal programs to the local level. It
makes no sense for Washington to tell Dubuque how to implement a
day-care program for county employees. Where local control has been
regained, schools have improved, welfare has been administered more
fairly, unemployment benefits are conditioned on job retraining and

temporary work assignments, and deadbeat fathers are held account-
able for child-support payments. In other words, programs are administered close to the needs of the community, making it a better place
to live.

A third essential to rebuilding a community atmosphere would be a resurgence
of volunteerism. No community can exist
today without a huge commitment of volunteers. For years we have been missionaries around the world, but today we must
turn our attention to our own communities. To volunteer in your neighborhood is
to say "I love this place!" Pride is restored
and problems are alleviated.

I'm happy to report that this is an area
where we are taking great strides.
Currently, more than 80 million
Americans volunteer their time or give
$120 billion in private donations to wor-
thy causes. More than 1.2 million people
work or volunteer for nonprofit organizations. Even with this level of commitment, the need for volunteer help will
increase dramatically in the next few
years, given federal cutbacks. By 2002, for
example, it is estimated that private giving
will need to increase 84 percent just to
make up for the loss of federal grants.

We can pick up the slack if you will:

*We must reward hard work and
individual merit and we must
hold individuals personally
responsible for their actions. And,
we must honor and preserve the
most important institution in
America, the very foundation of
our society—the family.*

GOVERNOR PETE WILSON
Sacramento, California

*The United States is recognized
and respected not because of its
industrial power or wealth but
by its moral and intellectual
accomplishments and contributions to mankind.*

ALEJANDRO ORFILA
Former Argentinian ambassador
to the United States
Secretary-general,
Organization of American States

- Pick a cause, one that you believe in with passion. Get involved.
  Give money and time. The odds are high that you'll get far more
  out of the experience than you will give to it. I have never met a
  community volunteer who didn't believe passionately in his or
  her cause.

- Help conquer illiteracy. If people can't read, they will never be able to fully participate in your community.
- Join with others to research what's happening in your community. It will help you identify causes in which you will have an interest. And be patient. Most community organizations are understaffed and underfinanced. Seek out those already using innovative approaches to problem-solving in your community. You will find some amazing efforts dealing with crime prevention, drug rehabilitation, youth programs, affordable housing, the homeless, school reform, and job training. Most are practical, and all need volunteers and financial support.
- Volunteer for a United Way agency or other service agency in your community. Give both time and money. You will be surprised to learn that many groups involved are on the leading edge of problem-solving. They can't survive, though, without help from people like you. Some of the most successful have included the Salvation Army, Goodwill Industries, and the American Red Cross.
- Give special attention to programs for disadvantaged kids. They'll never get off the vicious cycle of welfare dependency without your help through such groups as the Big Brothers/Big Sisters, Boy Scouts, Girl Scouts, local youth centers, YMCA family centers, Boys Clubs, and Girls Clubs.
- Encourage your kids to volunteer. Helping others is a key value you can pass along to the next generation. Today, more than thirteen million teenagers volunteer an average of 3.9 hours a week, according to a recent Gallup survey. Isn't that spectacular? The survey showed that the most important reason teenagers volunteer is that they want to do something useful.
- Get involved with a local school, whether you have children there or not. Principals and teachers need help. They are the only role models some of their students will ever have. In the next decade there will be a revolution in education, starting with better teaching, tougher discipline, and a values-centered envi-

ronment to help kids who have no role models at home. Corporations, churches and synagogues, and local service clubs are adopting schools to supplement their needs and to give encouragement to needy students everywhere.

- Encourage teaching as a career. Today, you are seeing thousands of sharp young college students, some from the top universities in America, selecting education as their profession. Some have volunteered for Teach for America, a marvelous teacher corps consisting of more than three thousand talented college graduates who commit two years to teaching in urban and rural public schools.

We Have Seen the Government, and It Is We

Good communities also require that we rethink our attitudes about government. It's popular today to beat up on the bureaucrats, but the fact is that our government departments are staffed by thousands of dedicated and talented men and women who have chosen such service for their careers. I support the idea of some level of mandatory public service for every young person. My generation grew up on the assumption that most physically fit males would enter the military, but we no longer have the draft to "motivate" that service. Often, time in the military was a life-defining experience, good and bad. A sense of community is dependent on many things, including those who are willing to devote their lives to public service. It's very important that we restore public service and politics as honorable, important lines of work.

On the Record

Coming from a state with the motto, "To the stars through difficulties," perhaps it's only natural that persistence is a value I consider to be of utmost importance. In a town known for rhetoric, I have a reputation for being a man of few words. But what words I say, I mean. And what promises I make, I keep.

SENATOR BOB DOLE
Republican, Kansas
Washington, D.C.

I would like to be known for my loyalty to my family and friends. I will stick by them through almost anything, not always agreeing but always there.

JAN TAYLOR
A community leader and
homemaker, Newnan, Georgia

Too many bright young leaders are unwilling to run for local office or get involved in the campaigns of others who share their views. Without a steady influx of unselfish, ethical men and women who are willing to serve for a time and then return to the private sector, we end up with the government we deserve. If we expect the best, we must encourage our best to get involved.

Here are some other ways to enhance our community spirit.

- Your most important community responsibility is to vote. In presidential election years, we're lucky if half the eligible voters make it to the polls, and in off-year elections even fewer voters show up. Democracy demands that you become involved. If you never vote or never support a candidate for office, then you have no right to complain from the sidelines.

- Call on your legislators or write them a letter. Learn how to communicate with them by fax and E-mail. Advocate your position on key issues. Let them know you are there, caring and watching. Legislators are keeping their ears very close to the ground these days. In many instances, those who haven't kept in touch have been thrown out of office, so what you have to say matters a whole lot.

- Support candidates and advocacy groups that represent those values key to your own life. Work on the campaign of a candidate who shares your beliefs. Handle the telephones, pass out brochures, open mail, raise money, put up signboards, organize neighborhood coffees. One thing we have learned in recent elections is that you can truly make a difference. There are almost one hundred new members of Congress to attest to that fact.

- Stay informed (read your local newspaper!). The best way for communities to grow and prosper is for everyone to know what's going on. You will have a hard time staying in your cocoon once you learn about the good and bad things that are happening in your community and that deserve your attention.

Good communities create a sense of belonging and a measure of security. They preserve traditions and values from generation to generation. Without them, families fall apart and people lose connection with one another. We can afford no less than your full involvement in your community.

One Nation, Under God

And, we must remember that our roots are anchored deep in a faith that attracted our forefathers to the shores of America. "We cannot read the history of our rise and development as a nation," Franklin Delano Roosevelt said, "without reckoning with the place the Bible has occupied in shaping the advances of the Republic."

It seems to me that we have two choices: give up or get involved. The first is unacceptable to those who care, but the alternative will require a level of personal commitment that goes far beyond what you have ever done before.

It's all up to you.

Chapter 17

Finish Strong

It's Never Too Soon, Never Too Late

But if a man happens to find himself, if he knows what he can be depended upon to do, the limits of his courage, the position from which he will no longer retreat, the extent of his dedication, then he has found a mansion which he can inhabit with dignity all the days of his life.

JAMES MICHENER
The Fires of Spring

Faith Keeper

My faith demands—this is not optional—that I do whatever I can, wherever I can, whenever I can, for as long as I can with whatever I have to try to make a difference.

FORMER PRESIDENT JIMMY CARTER

This book has been far tougher to write than I ever imagined. Like you, I have read hundreds of books over the years, and I don't think I ever appreciated the amount of work that went into each of those books. Quite frankly, there were times when I wanted to just walk away from my computer and leave the writing of books to others.

But I kept thinking of George Bush and his advice to me several years ago: "Above all, Dick, finish strong." I recalled his long public-service career spanning a half-century: a Navy fighter pilot in World War II, a congressman, director of the Central Intelligence Agency, vice president, and then president. In both victory and defeat, he started strong and finished strong. Now he has started over again—this time he's in the "grandfather business," as he likes to say. He'll do well in that line of work too, because he and his wife, Barbara, have never taken on a challenge without enthusiasm and determination.

I like that approach, and commend it to you. You don't have to just go through the motions, wherever you are in life. With a commitment to do your best, no matter what the odds, you will be a winner and this world will be just a little bit better because of you. People who give more than they are asked always seem to have more energy, while those who do just enough to get by seem to be so lethargic. Their lives are full of drudgery. How sad, because life doesn't have to be such a drag. You have a choice in how you live.

You Are Not Alone

I wrote this book to call attention to an alarming trend and to point us toward the kinds of values and attitudes that will make us great again. Yet there is a final area I need to address. It would be logical for you to conclude that all you need to do is work harder or be better—and I certainly support every effort toward self-improvement. But even those efforts won't work unless you realize you can't do it alone. In fact, the rugged individualism that played an important role in the development of our society has been taken to the extreme, thus contributing to our decline. In short, you can't do it alone. We need each other; we need to be part of something bigger than we are.

When the mythological Greek hero Odysseus went off to fight the Trojan War, he asked his close friend Mentor to care for his young son. It was a major responsibility, one that Mentor took very seriously. He served as the boy's constant companion, teaching him about life and personal responsibility. He was a good teacher and strong role model. To this day, in honor of this good man, we use the word *mentor* to describe a wise and faithful counselor.

Each of us has mentors in life. I would not be where I am today without mine. Many of them are quoted in the "On the Record" features of this book. I have never believed that there is any such thing as a self-made person. Every one of us is influenced by the inspiration of others. I hope you, too, have mentors—a special group of friends and family who have helped mold your values and clarify your goals. If you do not, you are missing out on a rich resource and your life will be incomplete. Being a rugged individual does not mean you do not seek the wise counsel of others. Somehow, we have gotten away from this important concept. Nothing I have recommended in this book will amount to much in your life if you do not apply it to your own life with the help of others. And to strengthen your own commitment, you need to pass on your own values as a mentor to others.

It's easy to become discouraged by the corruption and loss of morality around us. Often we feel helpless. We wonder if things can ever turn around. It may be tough to change our leaders, but we can influence some of the bright young people coming along. First, we need to help them focus on certain key personal values, starting with our ultimate dependence upon the Lord to guide us. Let's think of it as:

The Higher Ground Check List

- Anchor your life to higher ground. Simply do the right thing.
- Live your life according to this higher calling—God's calling.
- Don't always look to others to set the moral example because

some won't. Only you can determine the key personal values that should guide your life.

- Demand that your leaders set an example. That's what leadership is all about.
- Conduct your personal life in an exemplary manner. If you can be a positive influence on just one person each day you will make an enormous contribution.
- Center your life on principle, not popularity. Today's hero can become tomorrow's bum.
- When you make mistakes admit to them, apologize and learn from the experience. Others may be willing to forgive you but don't forget that you must accept the consequences of your actions.
- Build trusting relationships, starting with your family and friends. Trust counts, big time.
- Don't put yourself in positions where anyone could even *think* that you are doing something wrong. Perceptions are as powerful as reality.
- Cherish your family, close friends and marriage. Each is key to a meaningful life.
- Be an encourager, especially to those without hope.
- Always be optimistic, even when you think our country is falling apart. We have a long history of improving from one generation to the next. Soon it will be your turn.
- Serve others. The spirit of volunteerism is key to our future.

These are goals and personal values each of us can embrace. In a way, this check list summarizes everything in this book. It can be an important road map for your own life.

One Last Thought

During the months I spent writing this book, I reflected many times on what others had told me in their "On the Record" comments. The significance of what they had to say forced me to think about myself and how I wanted to be remembered. The answer came down to two simple thoughts:

> *Above all, I'd like to be known as a person who cherished his family and as a cheerful optimist who has encouraged others to do their best.*

That, in the end, is the overriding message I'd like to leave with you. Do your best, and do so with cheerfulness and optimism.

One of the more wholesome movies I have seen in a long time is *Mr. Holland's Opus,* that wonderful story about a dedicated teacher who struggled to write a symphony while teaching high school. After serving as a mentor to thousands of young people, Mr. Holland (brilliantly played by Richard Dreyfuss) was forced to retire owing to cuts in the music budget. Unbeknown to him, hundreds of his present and former students gathered in the school auditorium to pay tribute and to hear his symphony performed for the first time. Few theatergoers could hold back their tears as the movie ended with a standing ovation from Mr. Holland's fans. They had learned so much and wanted to say thank you.

I'll never forget the words of one of Mr. Holland's former students: "Mr. Holland, you have written the symphony, but we are your music."

You may never be able to finish as dramatically as Mr. Holland did. Real life and each of its chapters along the way don't always end as they do on the big screen. But you can become just as powerful an example to others, starting with your own family. It really doesn't matter how old you are, what job you have, or how much money you have. You can become part of a growing army of citizens who can change the world by the power of your example.

Seeking the Invocations of Life

Years ago, Hubert Humphrey inspired millions with his courageous fight against cancer. "Adversity is an experience, not a final act," he once said. "Some people look upon any setback as the end. They are always looking for the benediction rather than the invocation." Earlier, after losing a bitter presidential election in 1968, he commented about writing his concession speech: "I told myself this has to be done right because it is the opening speech of my next campaign."

So now it is time for an invocation. This isn't the final chapter of a book, but the first speech of your next campaign. There will be those who won't believe you can change, who will accuse you of being a "do-gooder" when they see you respond positively to challenges in your life. The first time you acknowledge any spiritual interest, they'll really let you have it. That's when you need to reach down deep within and connect with the desire that I believe God puts within each of us: The desire to make a difference, to be significant. The desire to leave a legacy that inspires those who follow.

When you were a child, you had big dreams. The world was a wonderful place to you, and you just knew you would grow up and make it better. In your teen years, you probably saw what adults were doing to this place and vowed you would never approach life the way they did. You would escape the rat race, be true to your spouse and children, never let your job own you, and always find adventure in every day.

Something happened along the way, and now you would like to undo the effects of letting your dreams slip away.

You can. My guess is that if you have made it this far in the book, you really do want to make the corrections necessary to get your life back on the upward journey. You agree that it is not what you own or where you live but *who you are* that counts. You have looked back on your life and discovered mentors who pointed you in the right direction, and more important, you see young faces looking up to you for guidance.

You started strong, maybe faltered a bit along the way, but now you want to make sure you hit the backstretch in full stride.

You can. Today. But only if you see it as a process and not another

> ### On the Record
>
> *Never let the challenge of a corrupt society corrupt your morals or sense of good values.*
>
> KEN CUTSHAW
> Attorney, Atlanta, Georgia
>
> *How long should a person live? I don't know. What's more important is how you live and what you live for.*
>
> FORMER VICE PRESIDENT
> HUBERT HUMPHREY

promise. We both have plenty of New Year's resolutions that never made it past January. What we need now is a new way of looking at life.

Let Your Light Shine

One of my favorite scripture passages is an account of the words of Jesus called the Sermon on the Mount. As Jesus tries to encourage His followers to live exemplary lives, He uses two metaphors: "You are the light of the world. A city on a hill cannot be hidden." Later He challenges: "Let your life shine before men." Those words became the basis for the old children's song "This Little Light of Mine."

As you head to work tomorrow; as you send your kids off to school; as you greet your spouse in the evening; as you work with a colleague in the office; as you drop your car off at the garage, remember.

The world needs your light.

Share Your Thoughts

I welcome input from the readers of this book, especially comments about what you read, ideas on how others can finish strong, steps we should take to uplift important personal values in life.

You also are encouraged to send me your own responses to the questions I posed with leaders included in the "On the Record" features of this book. Simply send your responses to the address noted below.

Personal Values Survey

1. What three accomplishments do you consider to be the most important in your life?
2. What three values would you like to be remembered for?
3. Who have been the two or three most important mentors to you and why? What did they teach you that will outlive your life?
4. Select one "unsung hero" whose values you admire; ordinary people who have done extraordinary things in their lives that show important personal values at their best.

Comments and responses should be sent to:

Richard G. Capen, Jr.
Box 2494
Rancho Santa Fe, CA 92067
Fax: (619) 756-1857
E-mail: rgcapen@aol.com

Acknowledgments

Woven throughout *Finish Strong* are references to people who have made an enormous difference in my life. Without their interest and inspiration, this book would not have been possible.

Above all, I am grateful to my family. For thirty-seven years my wife, Joan, has been a part of everything significant in my life. She has been the anchor for our family, starting of course with our three children, who are central to everything important to us. The book is dedicated to them.

My mother, Virginia Knowles Hufbauer, has been a determined lady of tremendous courage, fighting frail health most of her life. Many of my important values have been gained from her example. The fullness of her life came in 1960 when she married Clyde Hufbauer, a gentle and modest person who brought great love and joy to our family. His three children, Karl, Gary, and Joyce, and my brother Dave and I have grown together as a very close family, especially in the years following Clyde's death in 1993. My mother died in 1997.

I also am grateful for Shirley Capen, who married my father in 1949 and brought him many years of happiness. In so doing, she added a special dimension of love in my life.

In addition, I thank the couple who share much of the credit for everything central to me: Joan's parents, Jim and Joanne Lambert, who have shown everyone the true meaning of love in a strong marriage. The Lamberts celebrated their 58th wedding anniversary a few weeks before Jim died in 1997.

Jim Copley, who died in 1973 after a long battle with cancer, gave me my first opportunity in the newspaper business. My next boss, Mel Laird, took a huge chance when he assigned me a key responsibility at the Pentagon—at the very tender age of thirty-two. I have never worked for a more dynamic leader. The Laird team still has reunions every few years.

My next career move was made possible by Alvah Chapman, who, as Knight Ridder's chief executive, brought me into what I consider to be the nation's finest media group. Alvah has an uncanny ability to inspire the best in others. And finally, President George Bush, who honored me as one of his envoys. It was an almost ideal match-up of my career experience and interests.

Then there are dozens of special friends who helped me along the way, far too many to mention here. I wish that I could salute them all. Several must be mentioned, however:

Jim Lawrence, the Marine Corps general who was my able deputy and wise counselor during my time at the Defense Department. Jim is the epitome of integrity and loyalty.

Judge Peter Fay, a highly respected Federal Court of Appeals judge, has been a very close friend for many years. I was honored to have him swear me in as ambassador.

Dante Fascell, who took the somewhat unprecedented step of walking me from the House of Representatives to the Senate so that he could present my nomination as ambassador.

Jim Batten, who was key to my joining Knight Ridder in 1979. He was the clear choice to head the company, which he did with dedication and unquestioned integrity. Jim died in 1995 after a long battle against cancer.

Jim Michener, who is every writer's hero, and mine too. Living in Miami to write *Caribbean*, this legend was a wonderful encourager during some of my newspaper battles.

John Gardner, who has been a mentor to hundreds, including me. No one has lived out his personal values with greater commitment.

And, importantly, Billy Graham, a friend for more than twenty-five years, and Dan Yeary, my pastor in Miami. Both have enriched my understanding of the Lord and the power of His Word. Each in his own way has proven the essentiality of humility and deep faith.

I particularly want to acknowledge my colleagues at *The Miami*

Herald. Thanks to them, our newspaper was ranked twice during my years there as one of the top ten newspapers in the country. I took great pride in their achievements . . . well, most of the time. Let's face it; there were moments when they gave their publisher strong doses of humility, with a few ulcers thrown in.

I also am grateful for three wonderful career women who were assistants to me during my years in the newspaper business: Carolee Carter, my longtime administrative assistant at *The Miami Herald,* and Barbara Nance and Linda Myrick, who worked with me at Copley Newspapers. They helped me finish strong each step of the way.

This book would not have been possible without the vision and persistence of Clayton Carlson, the talented and universally respected publisher at Harper San Francisco, and Lyn Cryderman, my editor at Zondervan. Clayton took an interest in my commitment to write about personal values, and he stuck with me despite delays caused by my unexpected assignment in Madrid and, later, by my own procrastination. Mercifully for Clayton, I ran out of excuses and the job is done. I have learned over the years that the secret to good writing is a superb editor. With Lyn Cryderman, I had the best. His constant encouragement and commitment to the values reflected in *Finish Strong* were both inspiring and reassuring.

For this special edition published by the Billy Graham Evangelistic Association, I want to express my deep gratitude to John Corts, BGEA president, and to Bill Conard, the group's direct mail manager. They and their Association colleagues have been important encouragers in the unselfish and totally dedicated spirit of the Graham ministry. Together, we give all the glory to the Lord of us all.

Index

About the Author

Dick Capen's career represents a unique blend of diplomacy and newspaper publishing, highlighted by tours as United States Ambassador to Spain and more than three decades in the newspaper business. Known for his commitment to personal values and a positive approach to life, he is a nationally recognized columnist, author, and speaker on contemporary trends in America.

For more than thirteen years the author served as a director and senior executive at Knight Ridder, Inc., one of the country's most respected media companies. For seven of those years, Dick was chairman and publisher of Knight Ridder's flagship newspaper, *The Miami Herald*, which received five Pulitzer Prizes during his stewardship. The newspaper also was selected twice by *Time* magazine and *Advertising Age* as one of the nation's top-ten dailies. Conversant in Spanish, Dick led efforts in 1985 to start *El Nuevo Herald*, which is now the largest and most successful Spanish-language daily in the United States.

During his years at the helm of *The Herald*, Dick wrote a Sunday column that was widely read in both English and Spanish. In 1989 he was named Knight Ridder's vice-chairman, a position he held until 1991.

Dick Capen interrupted his newspaper career twice for tours in the federal government. His first appointment was in 1968 in the Department of Defense, where he served as Deputy Assistant Secretary of Defense and Assistant to the Secretary for Legislative Affairs. In 1971 he received the department's highest civilian decoration, the Distinguished Service Medal, for his leadership on prisoner-of-war matters and congressional liaison.

In 1992–93 Dick Capen served as United States Ambassador to Spain, where he led efforts to expand business opportunities and educational exchanges. Dick also served as chairman of the U.S. delegation to the 1992 Olympics in Barcelona.

In 1991 Dick chose to leave the newspaper business so that he could devote more time as an author and speaker on personal values essential to life. He serves as an independent director of Carnival Corporation, Freedom Communications, and two American Funds (New Economy and SmallCap). He served as a director of Knight Ridder, Inc., for eight years and is a past director of Purolator Services, Inc., the San Diego Trust Bank, and the United Press International.

On a pro bono basis, Dick has continued to assist in the promotion of business, trade, and educational exchanges between the United States and Spain. The Capens sponsor several scholarships awarded each year to outstanding students in Spain as an encouragement for them to study in the United States.

Born in Connecticut, Dick Capen is a graduate of Columbia University, which he attended on a Navy ROTC scholarship. He and his wife, Joan, who is a graduate of Westminster Seminary, have three grown children. They live in Rancho Santa Fe, California.

Steps to Peace with God

Step 1 — God's Purpose: Peace and Life

God loves you and wants you to experience peace and life—abundant and eternal.

The Bible Says . . .

". . . we have peace with God through our Lord Jesus Christ." Romans 5:1

"For God so loved the world that He gave His only begotten Son, that whoever believes in Him should not perish but have everlasting life." John 3:16

". . . I have come that they may have life, and that they may have it more abundantly." John 10:10b

Since God planned for us to have peace and the abundant life right now, why are most people not having this experience?

Step 2 — Our Problem: Separation

God created us in His own image to have an abundant life. He did not make us as robots to automatically love and obey Him, but gave us a will and a freedom of choice.

We chose to disobey God and go our own willful way. We still make this choice today. This results in separation from God.

Our choice results in separation from God.

The Bible Says . . .

"For all have sinned and fall short of the glory of God." Romans 3:23

"For the wages of sin is death, but the gift of God is eternal life in Christ Jesus our Lord." Romans 6:23

People (Sinful) — God (Holy)

Our Attempts

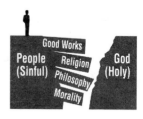

There is only one remedy for this problem of separation.

Through the ages, individuals have tried in many ways to bridge this gap . . . without success . . .

The Bible Says . . .

"There is a way that seems right to man, but in the end it leads to death." Proverbs 14:12

"But your iniquities have separated you from God; and your sins have hidden His face from you, so that He will not hear." Isaiah 59:2

Step 3 God's Remedy: The Cross

Jesus Christ is the only answer to this problem. He died on the Cross and rose from the grave, paying the penalty for our sin and bridging the gap between God and people.

The Bible Says . . .

". . . God is on one side and all the people on the other side, and Christ Jesus, Himself man, is between them to bring them together . . ." 1 Timothy 2:5

"For Christ also has suffered once for sins, the just for the unjust, that He might bring us to God . . ." 1 Peter 3:18a

"But God demonstrates His own love for us in this: While we were still sinners, Christ died for us." Romans 5:8

God has provided the only way . . . we must make the choice . . .

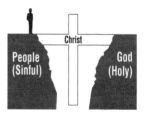

Step 4 Our Response: Receive Christ

We must trust Jesus Christ and receive Him by personal invitation.

The Bible Says . . .

"**Behold, I stand at the door and knock. If anyone hears My voice and opens the door, I will come in to him and dine with him, and he with Me.**" **Revelation 3:20**

"**But as many as received Him, to them He gave the right to become children of God, even to those who believe in His name.**" **John 1:12**

"**. . . if you confess with your mouth the Lord Jesus and believe in your heart that God has raised Him from the dead, you will be saved.**" **Romans 10:9**

Are you here . . . or here?

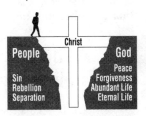

Is there any good reason why you cannot receive Jesus Christ right now?

How to receive Christ:

1. Admit your need (I am a sinner).
2. Be willing to turn from your sins (repent).
3. Believe that Jesus Christ died for you on the Cross and rose from the grave.
4. Through prayer, invite Jesus Christ to come in and control your life through the Holy Spirit. (Receive Him as Lord and Savior.)

What to Pray:

Dear Lord Jesus,

    I know that I am a sinner and need Your forgiveness. I believe that You died for my sins. I want to turn from my sins. I now invite You to come into my heart and life. I want to trust and follow You as Lord and Savior.

In Jesus' name. Amen.

_____   _____
Date   Signature

God's Assurance:
His Word

If you prayed this prayer,
The Bible Says...

"For 'whoever calls upon the name of the Lord will be saved.'" **Romans 10:13**

Did you sincerely ask Jesus Christ to come into your life? Where is He right now? What has He given you?

"For it is by grace you have been saved, through faith—and this is not from yourselves, it is the gift of God—not by works, so that no one can boast." Ephesians 2:8,9

The
Bible Says...

"He who has the Son has life; he who does not have the Son of God does not have life. These things I have written to you who believe in the name of the Son of God, that you may know that you have eternal life, and that you may continue to believe in the name of the Son of God." 1 John 5:12–13, NKJV

Receiving Christ, we are born into God's family through the supernatural work of the Holy Spirit who indwells every believer...this is called regeneration or the "new birth."

This is just the beginning of a wonderful new life in Christ. To deepen this relationship you should:

1. Read your Bible every day to know Christ better.
2. Talk to God in prayer every day.
3. Tell others about Christ.
4. Worship, fellowship, and serve with other Christians in a church where Christ is preached.
5. As Christ's representative in a needy world, demonstrate your new life by your love and concern for others.

God bless you as you do.

Billy Graham

If you want further help in the decision you have made, write to:
Billy Graham Evangelistic Association P.O. Box 779, Minneapolis, Minnesota 55440-0779